Genesis 1 ·

MW01169131

The Schoolmaster's Study: Book 1

By Robert S. Barber

May this humble work bless you as you grow up into Christ

Pastor Bob
The Schoolmaster

Mark —
Thanks to you and Sandy Core for 22 years of ministry and blessing to our family —
Bob & Ann Marie Barber

All Scripture quotations are from The Holy Bible, English Standard Version (ESV) copyright ©2001 Wheaton: Standard Bible Society

Table of Contents

Introduction 1

In the Beginning 3

Something from Nothing 5

When God Speaks..7

Things That Are Above 9

God's Good Earth...11

God's Great Garden 13

The Heavens Declare His Glory 15

God Loves Company 17

All God's Creatures; Great and Small...........................19

Made Like Him 21

God's Purpose and Design for the Family 23

It Was Very Good 25

The Day God Rested...27

God's Breath of Life 29

Two Trees...31

The River of Eden...33

Rest, Responsibility, and Rule of Paradise 35

Eden's First Lesson..37

The First Wedding..39

Rising Up from the Fall...41

The Blindness of Eden..43

When God Asks...45

Victory over Temptation Revealed in the Serpent's Curse 47

Sin's Consequences and God's Discipline 49

Clothed in His Righteousness...51

Back to the Tree of Life 53

Victory Over Sin 55

God's Tough Questions 57

Two Cities..59

God's Law Written on Our Hearts...61

Worthy of Our Trust and Devotion 63

God Rewards Those Who Seek Him...64

The Sovereignty and Mercy of God 66

The Blessings of Walking with God 68

How Do You Spell R-E-L-I-E-F? 70

Truth About gods and the Gospel Revealed in Genesis.............72

Grieved Him to His Heart 74

Find Favor in the Eyes of God 76

Hear and Obey God's Word 77

Living in the Covenant and Providence of God.........................79

Escape from a Stubborn World...81

Truth that Saved Even the Animals...82

God's Patience, Perfecting, and Protection 84

Choosing Life is as Simple as A, B, C.......................................86

But God Remembers..88

Ravens, Doves, and Serving God..90

Go Out from the Ark 92

God Still Responds to Evil Hearts 94

God Values Life 96

Children of the Covenant...98

The Pattern of Enslavement 100

The Only True King..102

Nothing is Impossible! 104

Our Sure Hope 106

Prepared for Greatness...108

Introduction

"And he gave the apostles, the prophets, the evangelists, the shepherds and teachers, to equip the saints for the work of ministry, for building up the body of Christ, until we all attain to the unity of the faith and of the knowledge of the Son of God, to mature manhood, to the measure of the stature of the fullness of Christ, so that we may no longer be children, tossed to and fro by the waves and carried about by every wind of doctrine, by human cunning, by craftiness in deceitful schemes. Rather, speaking the truth in love, we are to <u>grow up in every way into him who is the head, into Christ</u>, from whom the whole body, joined and held together by every joint with which it is equipped, when each part is working properly, makes the body grow so that it builds itself up in love" (Ephesians 4:11-16).

Life in Christ is a wonderful yet challenging journey through this difficult world as we eagerly anticipate the eternal life to come. The trials and temptations of this life take on meaning and purpose when we view them through the lens of God's Word. According to the Bible, this life is preparing us for eternal life. There are lessons to be learned in the confusion and chaos of here and now that will make perfect sense in eternity. The Biblical truth is that while we tarry here, we are to *grow up into Christ* more and more every day.

Our spiritual growth requires nourishment. The Spirit teaches this truth with the words, *"Man does not live by bread alone, but man lives by every word that comes from the mouth of the LORD"* (Deuteronomy 8:3). It is the truth that is found in God's Word that nourishes, encourages, and heals our spirit, and empowers our spiritual growth in Christ.

Here in Genesis, Moses records the beginning of everything. As truth seekers study this book of beginnings, the Spirit of Truth reveals the purpose behind everything God created. Here truth seekers will find the answers to life's basic questions: Where did we come from? Where are we going? Why are we here? What is right and what is wrong? What is good and what is bad? What is life and what is death? And so much more! Studying God's creation from its very beginning with the Spirit as our teacher and guide is a great way to follow Christ's invitation to get to know Him better... *"And this is eternal life, that they know you the only true God, and Jesus Christ whom you have sent"* (John 17:3).

As a fellow disciple of Jesus Christ, I am blessed to share this journey of growth in Christ with you. As a pastor, I pray that as I share some of the truth God has revealed to me as I've feasted on His Word, you will be built up and equipped as part of His body, the Church. And as a schoolmaster, I pray that the truth shared here will help you come to know and become more like Jesus Christ, *"in whom are hidden all the treasures of wisdom and knowledge"* (Colossians 2:3).

Totus Gloria ut Deus!
Pastor Bob
The Schoolmaster

In the Beginning

"In the beginning, God created the heavens and the earth" **(Genesis 1:1).**

Genesis: The book of beginnings. Very obviously, Genesis is the record of the beginning or the start of everything. But more than a historical record, The Spirit of Truth reveals God's never-changing truth about life's most controversial issues here. As the Holy Spirit inspired the prophet Moses to write these words for us, He reveals God's truth about life, death, sin, consequences, sacrifice, redemption, marriage, family, and so much more in the first eleven chapters of this book of beginnings. Because our spiritual growth requires nourishment from the truth found in God's Word, Genesis is a great place to begin to *grow up into Christ.*

God's creative work begins *in the beginning,* in fact, God created *the beginning.* But this truth begs the question, where was God before the beginning? One sarcastic philosopher of Augustine's day answered this question with, "God was preparing Hell for those who seek to pry into such things". But for the genuinely interested, there is certainly a more relevant and accurate answer.

You see, in order for God to initiate a beginning, He had to be the only one around. He has said, *"Earth is My footstool and Heaven is My throne"* **(Isaiah 66:1).** God did not need either a stool for His feet or a throne for His body. While both the heavens and the earth need Him as their Creator and Sustainer, He does not need them at all. In eternity God has always been and always will be sufficient and content in Himself. Where was God before the beginning? He was with the Son and the Holy Spirit. God needed neither angels nor men for fellowship or fulfillment. He was complete and content as the Three-in-One.

A better question now comes to mind... Where will you be after the end? Oh yes, because you are created in His image **(see Genesis 1:26-27),** like Him you are meant to live forever. The only question is where will you live forever? It comes into focus now... God created the heavens and the

3

earth as a home for Himself, the angels, and those He would choose to share the blessedness He has known in eternity. His purpose for creation has not changed. He still longs to share the sweet fellowship He has always known as Father, Son, and Holy Spirit with you. In fact, because He lives forever, God's desire to be close to you is as earnest now as it was...

In the Beginning.

Something from Nothing

"The earth was without form and void, and darkness was over the face of the deep. And the Spirit of God was hovering over the face of the waters" (Genesis 1:2).

There are three very beautiful and precious truths here in the record of the beginning of creation. But to grasp these truths we have to eliminate some blinding traditions and assumptions. We cannot see or understand these encouraging truths if we do not accept that God created the heavens and the earth. Moreover, we cannot know and enjoy the blessings of these truths unless we accept that everything God created is good. Most of us have spent hours studying creation in secular classrooms from a humanistic point of view. Too many Christian parents are still perpetuating a blinding worldview by immersing their children (God's kids) in the same blindness. But as we trust Jesus Christ to renew our soul at rebirth, we can trust him now to renew our mind to receive His precious truth as revealed even at the very beginning of beginning.

The first truth is God created the earth *without form and void*. Literally, God created the earth as *tohu* (Hebrew); desolate, deserted, empty, and worthless. He created the earth as *bohu* (Hebrew); barren, empty, ruined, and vacant. By common standards, this does not sound good. But remember, God decides what is good and what is evil. In beginning creation without form and void, God demonstrates how He can bring forth beauty and order from the deepest emptiness and chaos.

The second truth is *darkness was over the face of the deep*. Darkness, *khoshek* (Hebrew); misery, destruction, death, ignorance, sorrow, wickedness. Again, from a humanistic perspective, darkness is evil and light is good. But if we accept God as creator of all, including darkness **(see Isaiah 45:7)** and judge of good and evil, and if we remember that He called everything He created good, we position our heart to receive a precious truth about darkness. It is good. Darkness is good when God is ruling over it. It's darkness that causes us to look up for light.

The third truth is *the Spirit of God was hovering over the face of the waters.* The Spirit of God was literally *rakaph* (Hebrew) brooding, moving, shaking over the waters. God had created an emptiness and darkness and He was willing to stay close to it. He was not detached from the chaos and misery that He brought into existence. He was in it and over it, preparing to do something spectacular through it.

You see, by beginning with emptiness and darkness God makes the point that He can create fulfillment and light out of anything or nothing. His Spirit is present in the deepest, darkest moments of our lives too. He's brooding there, shaking with eagerness to bring fulfillment and meaning out of emptiness and darkness. It's in the chaos and darkness that God allows to cover us and overwhelm us so deeply at times that we become aware that His Spirit is compelling us to look to Jesus Christ, the Light and Life of the world! As you and your children *grow up into Christ*, may you experience the special ways that God creates...

Something from Nothing.

When God Speaks

"And God said, 'Let there be light,' and there was light. And God saw that the light was good. And God separated the light from the darkness. God called the light Day, and the darkness he called Night. And there was evening and there was morning, the first day" (Genesis 1:3-5).

To receive the Biblical truth proclaimed here we must set aside our carnal worldview. We must take a moment to ask the Author of these words, the Holy Spirit, to clear our hearts and minds and to make us receptive to His truth. God wants to speak to us here, and He shows us here that when God speaks, great things happen!

Notice how God created here. God spoke. God speaks just like we do, for we are created like Him. He forms letters and words into sentences and paragraphs. Do your children's teachers remind them daily as they are laboring through spelling, vocabulary, and grammar that they are imitating God, who made them like Him so they can communicate with Him as well as with others? Do they learn that when they write sentences, paragraphs, stories, and more that they are creating and communicating ideas in this orderly, understandable way because they are reflecting the creativity, order, and relationship characteristics of God? God's kids deserve this kind of Biblical education because it is built on His truth and it helps them to think Biblically as they *grow up into Christ.*

Today's text also reveals that God speaks in a much more powerful way than we do. Just like God, we arrange letters, words, sentences, paragraphs, stories, and more to create and communicate ideas, but God actually speaks real things into being. Because we live in a world corrupted by sin our creativity is limited to speaking about and naming ideas and things that already exist. But when God speaks, things that do not exist become real. We should always remember that when God hears our words, He sees the realities they represent. Do our words bless God? Are we and our children using our words here on earth to prepare us to use our words in a glorious and creative way in eternity?

How wonderful to learn from scripture today that the first reality God spoke into existence was light. In the previous verse we noted that God began creation with darkness covering everything. Here He speaks the reality of light into existence in order to illuminate His soon-to-come acts of creation. He wants us to see and be a part of His creative work. He wants to share everything with us. What a precious foreshadow of what He has done for us through the Son... ***"He has delivered us from the domain of darkness and transferred us to the kingdom of his beloved Son, in whom we have redemption, the forgiveness of sins"*** **(Colossians 1:13-14).** As we *grow up into Christ* may we learn to use our words in a way that reflects the truth that light and goodness are among the wonderful realities that result...

When God Speaks.

Things That Are Above

"And God said, 'Let there be an expanse in the midst of the waters, and let it separate the waters from the waters.' And God made the expanse and separated the waters that were under the expanse from the waters that were above the expanse. And it was so. And God called the expanse Heaven. And there was evening and there was morning, the second day" (Genesis 1:6-8).

May God empty us of the foolish understanding, tradition, and perspectives of the world that have infiltrated our hearts and minds. May God transform our minds as we examine His Word and prepare our hearts to receive and trust His truth in a fresh way today.

On the second day of creation, God began a work of separation and preparation. Out of all the elements He fashioned two areas and separated them with an expanse we call the sky. He gave a name to the arena above, Heaven. He left the arena below nameless for now because He has much more to do there in order to prepare it as a home for His very special creatures, man and woman.

The waters above the expanse are of the same substance as the waters below, yet they are gathered and separated from the water below. They are placed in a particular location above the waters below. This process reveals some very important Biblical truth. Heaven does not gather and stand firmly in place all by itself. Heaven is separated from Earth by a vast expanse and stands firm through the Word of God. Heaven is a very real and physical place. It is high above and separated from the physical world we live in. And Heaven exists today. It was created by God in the beginning and has existed as long as Earth.

Once we have grasped the truth about Heaven we should begin to understand why philosophies created by man and centered on man (humanism) reject the very existence of Heaven. To accept Heaven as defined here in today's text, one must accept that because God alone created Heaven and because He alone separated and now sustains the vast expanse between Heaven and Earth, it is only God who can create a way to overcome this expanse and get to Heaven. To accept Biblical truth about Heaven, we must believe in and trust God.

As believers, we must be discerning and wary of worldly philosophies, speculations, and traditions that deny the existence of life after death, Heaven and Hell. And we should certainly keep our children, God's kids, from being immersed in such foolishness as it obviously distracts their hearts and minds away from God and limits their understanding to things below, here on Earth. This makes it difficult for them to believe in and trust God. As we and our children *grow up into Christ* we should **(see Colossians 3:1-2)** keep our hearts and minds set on the sure and certain...

Things That Are Above.

God's Good Earth

"And God said, 'Let the waters under the heavens be gathered together into one place, and let the dry land appear.' And it was so. God called the dry land Earth, and the waters that were gathered together he called Seas. And God saw that it was good" **(Genesis 1:9-10).**

Lord, grant us faith to understand that the universe was created by Your Word **(see Hebrews 11:3).** Grant us spiritual wisdom to learn from what You created as well as to learn from the way You created. Please remove any strongholds that may exist in our understanding because of the influence of worldly traditions and foolishness. May our minds be renewed and our hearts be transformed by Your Word today **(see Romans 12:2)**!

Did you catch it? In His first work on this day two of creation, when God separated the waters with a great expanse into two bodies, He named that expanse Heaven. He then separated the lower waters, gathering them together into one place, and He named the dry land that divided the waters Earth. But he reserved His declaration that it was good for the latter work. He specifically labeled the separation of waters and the emergence of Earth as good. He did not say the same about the creation of the firmament we call Heaven. The Holy Spirit reveals important Biblical truth here that we and our children will miss if He is not our Teacher as we study God's creation.

God calls the dividing of the waters and the emergence of dry land good, even though there was nothing at all existing either on the land or in the waters. The Earth was barren and the Sea was empty. Yet this seemingly insignificant act is declared good by Almighty God because He was so excited about the beginning of His most beautiful work, the preparation of a home for us.

The Biblical truth is that God shows more concern on this second day of creation about our dwelling place than His own. He places priority and value on life with Him here on Earth, encouraging us not to be consumed with what it will be like in Heaven. We are not to become *so Heavenly minded that we are no Earthly good.* He calls us to learn to be content with small beginnings and with His perfect provision here while we are being prepared to join Him one day there. He challenges us to be about His work here on Earth even as we keep our hearts and minds set on things above. As you and your loved ones *grow up into Christ,* may you be ever thankful for His provision and ever blessed as you are about His work right here on...

God's Good Earth.

God's Great Garden

"And God said, 'Let the earth sprout vegetation, plants yielding seed, and fruit trees bearing fruit in which is their seed, each according to its kind, on the earth.' And it was so. The earth brought forth vegetation, plants yielding seed according to their own kinds, and trees bearing fruit in which is their seed, each according to its kind. And God saw that it was good. And there was evening and there was morning, the third day" (Genesis 1:11-13).

If we're willing to seek the truth, we'll learn some important facts about God as we examine the third day of creation today. Here, the Holy Spirit reveals the omnipotence, wisdom, and benevolence of God.

By His Word God created so many beautiful and useful plants and trees. In an instant, and by His Word He made the whole dry land fertile with a rich variety of vegetation that would be food and so much more for the creatures and human beings that would follow shortly. Through this third-day chapter of the creation story God's omnipotence is revealed. Those who teach other, less substantiated theories of origins and beginnings deny the truth of God's omnipotence and reject the power of His Word.

The incredible variety and diversity of plant life created by God reveals His wisdom. No human mind could possibly imagine, let alone create such lovely, varied, and useful plant life. The colors, textures, tastes, and powers of so many herbs, shrubs, vines, trees, and plants, all reveal wisdom beyond the capabilities of the human mind. Honest study of plant life and the marvelous way that plants compliment the rest of creation and reproduce after their own kind still reveals God's wisdom to students of truth today.

The timing of God's creation of plant life also reveals His great benevolence. God spoke plants into existence before He created the sun and allowed the rain to nourish and sustain them. God Himself was the caretaker of the first garden. Plants depended solely on the Creator to provide everything they would need to thrive and reproduce. Truth-seeking study of the Earth's complicated yet regular patterns of climate and weather reveals that God still cares for His entire creation.

I pray that you are encouraged by God's omnipotence, wisdom, and benevolence as revealed in Moses' record of this third day of creation. I pray you are motivated to see that your children, God's kids are taught by Christ-following teachers in Biblically-founded schools where they enjoy discovering and trusting His truth every day as they study His creation. As you and your loved ones *grow up into Christ* may you be reminded of and experience His omnipotence, wisdom, and benevolence every day as you enjoy the bounty of...

God's Great Garden.

The Heavens Declare His Glory

"And God said, 'Let there be lights in the expanse of the heavens to separate the day from the night. And let them be for signs and for seasons, and for days and years, and let them be lights in the expanse of the heavens to give light upon the earth.' And it was so. And God made the two great lights—the greater light to rule the day and the lesser light to rule the night—and the stars. And God set them in the expanse of the heavens to give light on the earth, to rule over the day and over the night, and to separate the light from the darkness. And God saw that it was good. And there was evening and there was morning, the fourth day" (Genesis 1:14-19).

May we be sensitive and receptive to the Holy Spirit as we seek God's truth today **(see John 16:13)**. There are three truths revealed by the record of Moses regarding God's creation of lights in the expanse He called Heaven. If we deny that God created the Heavens and the Earth, we miss these very encouraging truths. It's indispensable to our spiritual growth that we learn God's truth, and He commands us to see that our children (His kids) are taught these truths as they study His creation **(see Deuteronomy 6:6-7)** because He wants to reveal Himself to them.

God created the sun, moon, and planets to be signs. He had not yet created any creature with the ability to read and understand signs. Here we see indisputable evidence that God created the universe as a home for human beings, created like Him and able to grasp glimpses of His nature and character whenever we humbly study the world and sky around us. The Holy Spirit declares, *"The heavens declare the glory of God, and the sky above proclaims his handiwork. Day to day pours out speech, and night to night reveals knowledge"* (Psalm 19:1-2). The heavenly bodies are created to be studied, not worshipped.

God created the sun, moon, and planets to rule over the day and night of earth. But we must not forget that because God created the heavenly bodies and set them in their place in the heavens, and continues to keep them safely on their courses by His Word, Jesus Christ **(see Colossians**

1:16-17), we are not ruled by them. They are ruled by Christ on our behalf. Serious, humble study of the stars reveals to genuine truth seekers Christ's magnificent sovereignty and providence as He cares for and protects our precious home here on Earth.

A deeper truth also emerges here. Science and religion are not incompatible for genuine truth seekers. Science is the comprehension or understanding of truth or facts by the mind. If we study creation in order to seek truth and know what is real, we will discover the Creator. We see here in Scripture that one of God's primary purposes for placing the sun, moon, and stars in the heavens is for us to study them that we might come to see His glory and know Him better. As you and your family *grow up into Christ,* studying God's creation, may you come to know Him better and better as...

The Heavens Declare His Glory.

God Loves Company

"And God said, 'Let the waters swarm with swarms of living creatures, and let birds fly above the earth across the expanse of the heavens.' So God created the great sea creatures and every living creature that moves, with which the waters swarm, according to their kinds, and every winged bird according to its kind. And God saw that it was good. And God blessed them, saying, 'Be fruitful and multiply and fill the waters in the seas, and let birds multiply on the earth.' And there was evening and there was morning, the fifth day" (Genesis 1:20-23).

God has said He does not speak in secret, but He speaks the truth clearly and openly **(see Isaiah 45:19).** If we are seeking truth, His Spirit will lead us to it **(see John 16:13).** God has revealed some wonderful truth here on the fifth day of creation as His Spirit moved Moses to record how He created the first swimming and flying creatures. The truth is in how God created as well as in what He created, and it's very encouraging!

The power and diversity of God is revealed in the marvelous variety of creatures that filled the sea and the air on this day of creation. In beginning with the sea and the air God showed that His intention was to fill creation, from its deepest depths to its highest heights with beautiful and useful creatures. Soon He would assign mankind to guard and care for these creatures. This reveals the truth that God intended for us to reflect and exercise His authority over the entirety of His creation. When we believe this and help our children to grasp the truth that God wants us to respect and care for all He has created as His stewards we are fulfilling His will.

The blessing of reproduction that God granted to His creatures reveals another precious truth about His character. God loves company. He could have created exactly the number of creatures He wanted. He could have numbered each species. Instead, He created the first of each species and placed within them the ability to reproduce *according to their kinds.* Then he commanded them to fill their habitations. The truth is God loves company and He loves to share His work with others. This truth encourages us to seek His will and to show our children how to do the same after us.

God wants us to marvel at and care for His creatures and His creation. He wants us to pass on a heritage of seeking His truth and doing His will to our children. As you and your children *grow up into Christ* may you also grow as stewards of His creation and be blessed by the truth that...

God Loves Company.

All God's Creatures; Great and Small

"And God said, 'Let the earth bring forth living creatures according to their kinds—livestock and creeping things and beasts of the earth according to their kinds.' And it was so. And God made the beasts of the earth according to their kinds and the livestock according to their kinds, and everything that creeps on the ground according to its kind. And God saw that it was good" (Genesis 1:24-25).

God shows that He has purpose in mind when He creates the living creatures to inhabit Earth. It wasn't simply for our use that he produced all these creatures. It was also for our benefit in the sense that we might see the overflowing abundance of his creatures and be overwhelmed at the Creator's power. God wants us to know that *All God's Creatures; Great and Small* (from a hymn by Cecil Alexander) were produced by His wisdom and love for the human being that He planned to create soon.

Further, God was planning for the crown of His creation, mankind **(see Psalm 8:5)** to enjoy and learn some precious truth from overseeing and caring for His creatures. He wanted to share the management and care of His creatures so that human beings would be close enough and involved enough with the animals to experience the blessedness He Himself knew even before He created them. Living in peace with and caring for the living things God created was always supposed to move us to appreciate the majesty, power, creativity, and benevolence of our great Creator.

Sin has corrupted the creation in many ways. After the fall, animals turned on each other and on man. Plants brought forth thorns and thistles and the earth resisted mankind's efforts to farm it. Worst of all, mankind inherited a sin nature that naturally rejects the truth that God created and cares for the world. But the wonderful truth is that God's plan remains untouched and unchanged by our sin. He still reveals Himself to genuine truth seekers who study and appreciate His creatures. His truth is still revealed to our children when they study His creatures and creation through the lens of His Word. As you and your children continue *to grow up into Christ,* may you be reminded daily of His great love and care for you by the diversity and variety of...

All God's Creatures; Great and Small.

Made Like Him

"Then God said, 'Let us make man in our image, after our likeness. And let them have dominion over the fish of the sea and over the birds of the heavens and over the livestock and over all the earth and over every creeping thing that creeps on the earth.' So God created man in his own image, in the image of God he created him; male and female he created them" (Genesis 1:26-27).

For those willing to let the Holy Spirit guide them into all truth **(see John 16:13),** there is indeed much truth here about God and mankind. If we think as the world does, we miss God's truth revealed here. When we see that our children, God's kids, are taught His truth about beginnings and the creation of humankind, we enable them to grasp some powerful life-shaping truth for themselves.

God said "let *us*... after *our*". God reveals that He is more than one person here. He reveals only a glimpse of Himself, but we know enough already to discern that He is three persons in one. We met God the Creator in **Genesis 1:1,** God the Spirit in **Genesis 1:2,** and God the Word in **Genesis 1:3** and several times after that during the work of creation. We'll come to know and understand the Trinity better as we let the Holy Spirit be our guide through the Word of God.

God created man (Hebrew, adam: the generic term for mankind which becomes the proper name *Adam* later) in His image: *tselem* and after His likeness: *demooth* (Hebrew; shadow, shade, resemblance). It's as if God cast His shadow over us at creation and left it there. Of course, for a shadow to exist there must be strong light and the object that casts the shadow must be nearby, between the light and the surface that receives the shadow.

The truth revealed here is that while God is very complex, existing as a Trinity, He shows how much He wants us know Him by placing His image within us. Whenever we look at each other or into a mirror, we are to see the likeness of our Creator. And, God's constant image *in* us is also intended to be the comfort of God's constant nearness *to* us. As you and your children, God's kids, grow up into Christ, may you be encouraged by the image and nearness of God seen in others because we are...

Made Like Him.

God's Purpose and Design for the Family

"And God blessed them. And God said to them, 'Be fruitful and multiply and fill the earth and subdue it, and have dominion over the fish of the sea and over the birds of the heavens and over every living thing that moves on the earth.'" (Genesis 1:28).

The answers to some basic questions about humanity are to be found by truth seekers in our text today. What is a family? Why did God create the family? What is the key to a successful, healthy marriage and family? We and our children must discern and apply the truthful answers found in God's Word to these questions if we are to build the kind of marriages and families God wants us to enjoy. Those who corrupt or deny the truth God reveals in this scripture, will find no support here for anything other than the traditional family founded on marriage between one man and one woman.

God planned a very simple yet profound relationship when He commanded the man and woman to be fruitful and multiply. He established clear differences between the man and the woman that would draw them together and toward Him as they sought to fulfill His command. The relationship between man and woman that would produce children reflects the same process observed already in the land. As the ground received and nourished seeds from plants and vegetation in order to reproduce plants, the woman was to receive and nourish seed from the man in order to reproduce the image of God in children.

God established marriage and family as the very first relationships of any kind in order to bring forth and grow up children. Through the family God was multiplying the image of Himself that He placed in humans and He was *"seeking Godly offspring"* (Malachi 2:15). And, even more, God promised that as families fulfilled His purpose, raising up and filling the earth with Godly children, humankind would subdue the earth and rule over all of His creation. One of the secrets to living victoriously over the circumstances of life is to be faithful in marriage and parenting, helping each other within the family to seek God's truth and to *grow up into Christ* as we fulfill...

God's Purpose and Design for the Family.

It Was Very Good

"And God said, 'Behold, I have given you every plant yielding seed that is on the face of all the earth, and every tree with seed in its fruit. You shall have them for food. And to every beast of the earth and to every bird of the heavens and to everything that creeps on the earth, everything that has the breath of life, I have given every green plant for food.' And it was so. And God saw everything that he had made, and behold, it was very good. And there was evening and there was morning, the sixth day" (Genesis 1:29-31).

Genuine truth seekers are rewarded with several very encouraging truths here in Moses' record of the conclusion of the sixth day of creation. Those who reject God as Creator and Sovereign over the universe will find much confusion and anxiety here. May the Holy Spirit guide us into the blessings of truth as we study God's Word today.

The first truth revealed here is that upon reflecting on all He created, God declared that *it was very good.* Notice that God did not ask the man for his opinion. There was no consultation, evaluation, or vote. God was the one-and-only judge of the condition of creation. His opinion was all that mattered.

The second truth is that with the words, *it was very good,* God established a standard. He set the bar. Again, there was no input from the man. God's standard of goodness was the highest and best because He created it according to His wisdom, which is higher than that of the man.

Finally, with God's judgment firmly established and settled over the creation, everything was in a perfectly blessed state. Things were very different and they have never been the same. Animals did not threaten and attack each other for food because in God's *very good* world, He provided food in great abundance through plants and vegetation. All of God's creatures, including the man, submitted to God's rule, wisdom, and care and as a result they enjoyed perfect health and peace.

While much about the creation has changed, God has not changed. When we pursue and submit to His wisdom and sovereignty over our lives we enjoy glimpses of His blessings today and we experience a taste of the complete and perfect blessings He has in store for us in eternity. As you and your loved ones *grow up into Christ,* may you come to know and trust in the goodness and sovereignty of God, who still echoes...

It Was Very Good.

The Day God Rested

"Thus the heavens and the earth were finished, and all the host of them. And on the seventh day God finished his work that he had done, and he rested on the seventh day from all his work that he had done. So God blessed the seventh day and made it holy, because on it God rested from all his work that he had done in creation" **(Genesis 2:1-3).**

God rested, *Shabat* (Hebrew: cease, celebrate). Placing an exclamation point on creation, *God rested.* Emphasizing that creation was *very good,* complete, and perfect in every way, *God rested.* Showing how pleased He was with all He had made, and how blessed He was to share it all with the man, *God rested.*

God did not take the day off. Rather, He ceased from doing the work of creation and He paused to celebrate and enjoy the finished work. Because we are made like Him, we too have a desire deep within us to pause and appreciate creation. When we study the universe and our planet with an honest desire to discover truth, we encounter clear evidence of the Creator because He has made everything to be a perfect and complete reflection of His truth. If we want our children, God's kids, to *grow up into Christ* as they spend 30-35 hours per week in schools studying God's creation, their teachers should encourage them to pause and celebrate the work God has called *very good* as He reveals His truth to them.

God rested on the seventh day and He also *made it holy.* God sanctified *qādash* (Hebrew: consecrated, dedicated, kept clean) this particular day of what would become our week as a day of rest for all of creation as well as for Himself. God wants us to develop the habit of resting in Him and celebrating His finished work. Keeping the Sabbath became a mark of the Israelites that distinguished them from other nations. The spiritual discipline of resting in the Lord and worshipping Him as Creator is now celebrated on the Lord's Day, the first day of the week, by Christ followers, in recognition of Christ's resurrection and the finished work of salvation. It remains a characteristic that sets true believers apart today and looks forward to the promise of rest in Him in eternity.

As you and your children *grow up into Christ* may you find rest in Him and His finished work as you grow in your celebration and appreciation of...

The Day God Rested.

God's Breath of Life

"These are the generations of the heavens and the earth when they were created, in the day that the Lord God made the earth and the heavens. When no bush of the field was yet in the land and no small plant of the field had yet sprung up—for the Lord God had not caused it to rain on the land, and there was no man to work the ground, and a mist was going up from the land and was watering the whole face of the ground—then the Lord God formed the man of dust from the ground and breathed into his nostrils the breath of life, and the man became a living creature" **(Genesis 2:4-7).**

Genesis, the book of beginnings, answers the basic questions about life. Today's text reveals important truth about human beings. Mankind is very much like the other creatures God created, but also very different.

People are like animals in that they have a body that is *formed* (Hebrew: yāṣar; fashioned out of, brought forth from) of the dust of the earth. A word from the same root was used when God said let the earth *bring forth* (Hebrew: yāṣā'; proceed from, come out of) the creatures of the land. Just like animals, humans have a body.

Unlike the animals, the first man had the *breath of life* (Hebrew: neshāmâ and ḥay; living wind, divine inspiration, intellect, soul) breathed into his body by God. Adam was separated from the animals because God breathed into him the ability to reason, to study, enjoy, and respond to God and His creation. God had already declared that human beings were to *fill the earth and subdue it and have dominion over it* **(see Genesis 1:28).** Now God breathed into us His grace in order to equip us to fulfill our divine purpose.

You can see how the theory of evolution has corrupted mankind's view of himself. If we believe we are descended from the animals then we have no reason or ability to rule over and care for them as God's stewards. If we are to assume our stewardship role in God's creation we must believe His truth, that we have hearts, minds, and wills that work together to enable us to seek, know, and obey God. If our children, God's kids, are to become disciples of Christ they should be taught by Christian teachers to discern and reject the lie that they are evolved randomly like the animals, and they must learn and grasp the truth that God has uniquely and wonderfully created them for a very special purpose. We and our children, God's kids, should be encouraged always to *grow up into Christ,* who breathed on the disciples as they received the Holy Spirit **(see John 20:22)** in order to reveal the truth that our bodies are meant to be filled with...

God's Breath of Life.

Two Trees

"And the Lord God planted a garden in Eden, in the east, and there he put the man whom he had formed. And out of the ground the Lord God made to spring up every tree that is pleasant to the sight and good for food. The tree of life was in the midst of the garden, and the tree of the knowledge of good and evil" **(Genesis 2:8-9).**

Every tree that God planted and nurtured in the Garden of Eden was pleasant to the sight and good for food. However, the Holy Spirit moved Moses to draw attention to two particular trees. God wanted us to remember forever the tree of life and the tree of the knowledge of good and evil. These two trees reveal some important truths about our relationship with God.

The tree of life reminds us that life is a gift of God. We are to trust God as provider of everything we need to live the life He's given us as a gift. Further, because God was the creator and nurturer of the tree of life, we know He is the one who defined the quantity and quality of life. Approaching the tree of life was to be an act of worship for Adam as he submitted to and trusted his Creator's providence of an abundant and eternal life. The tree of life pointed forward to the tree where, *"He himself bore our sins in his body on the tree, that we might die to sin and live to righteousness"* **(1 Peter 2:24).** When we approach that tree, Calvary's cross, in faith, we receive forgiveness and we are restored to abundant and eternal life once again.

The tree of the knowledge of good and evil reminds us that God is the ultimate judge of good and evil. Approaching the tree of the knowledge of good and evil was also to be an act of worship for Adam as he submitted to God as the ultimate judge of good and evil. God wanted Adam to trust Him and to seek His righteousness. The tree of the knowledge of good and evil also pointed forward to eternity when, *"The Lord will show the nations of the world his justice; all will praise him. His righteousness shall be like a budding tree"* **(Isaiah 61:11).** When we approach that tree, the righteousness of God, in humility and faith, we receive the grace to

31

live righteously in this unrighteous world as we look forward to living forever in His Kingdom of Righteousness.

As you and your family *grow up into Christ,* may you enjoy the blessings of abundant, eternal, and righteous life reflected in the Garden of Eden by God's...

Two Trees.

The River of Eden

"A river flowed out of Eden to water the garden, and there it divided and became four rivers. The name of the first is the Pishon. It is the one that flowed around the whole land of Havilah, where there is gold. And the gold of that land is good; bdellium and onyx stone are there. The name of the second river is the Gihon. It is the one that flowed around the whole land of Cush. And the name of the third river is the Tigris, which flows east of Assyria. And the fourth river is the Euphrates" (Genesis 2:10-14).

Just as the river of Eden nourished and cleansed the garden, may the Holy Spirit nourish and cleanse our hearts and minds as we seek God's truth in His Word today.

The river of Eden is a reminder that God is Sustainer as well as Creator of everything. He remains intimately involved as Provider of all that creation needs to flourish. It's no wonder that Jeremiah described God as *"the LORD, the fountain of living water"* (Jeremiah 17:13). Zechariah prophesied that when Jesus returns and throughout His millennial reign here on the earth, *"Living waters shall flow out from Jerusalem, half of them to the eastern sea and half of them to the western sea. It shall continue in summer as in winter"* (Zechariah 14:8).

God showed John a river like the river of Eden that will be restored in eternity... *"Then he showed me the river of living water, sparkling like crystal, flowing from the throne of God and of the Lamb down the middle of the broad street of New Jerusalem. The tree of life was on both sides of the river, bearing twelve kinds of fruit, producing its fruit every month. The leaves of the tree are for healing the nations, and there will no longer be any curse"* (Revelation 22:1-3).

Jesus offers truth seekers a taste of His *living waters* today... *"'Whoever believes in me, as the Scripture has said, out of his heart will flow rivers of living water.' Now this he said about the Spirit, whom those who believed in him were to receive"* (John 7:38-39).

33

Jesus' offer remains in place today. After we've trusted Him to atone for our sin, our hearts become the dwelling place of His Holy Spirit. As we *grow up into Christ* and we're nourished by His Spirit, may our hearts be filled and those close to us be sprinkled by the overflowing of His living waters, just as the garden and neighboring lands were watered by...

The River of Eden.

Rest, Responsibility, and Rule of Paradise

"The Lord God took the man and put him in the Garden of Eden to work it and keep it. And the Lord God commanded the man, saying, 'You may surely eat of every tree of the garden, but of the tree of the knowledge of good and evil you shall not eat, for in the day that you eat of it you shall surely die'" **(Genesis 2:15-17).**

Three indispensable Biblical truths are revealed here for truth seekers. May the Lord help us to grasp and apply them today. God *rested* Adam in the garden even as he was to work there. Adam's responsibilities in the garden revealed that there was *danger in Paradise.* Adam's enjoyment of Paradise and participation in God's plan depended upon his obedience to one *rule.*

God *put* (Hebrew: *nuach;* rested, gave rest, calm, comfort) Adam in the garden to work it and keep it. Although Adam now had responsibilities and work to do every day, the truth revealed here is that his work was not toilsome and laborious. In fact, God intended for Adam to discover rest and comfort in his work. When we pursue and perform the Lord's will and work we find fulfillment and rest. This truth should compel us to see that our children are immersed in God's truth as they are prepared to discern and pursue His *"good and pleasing, and perfect will"* **(see Romans 12:2)** for their lives.

God put Adam in the garden to *work it* (Hebrew: *abad;* serve, cultivate) and to *keep it* (Hebrew: guard, keep watch, defend, protect). While everything God created was perfect and good, Paradise was to be guarded against some unseen danger or enemy here. We are reminded here that believers have to be constantly on guard, cultivating and protecting our faith and fellowship with God against all who would seek to attack us. Our children, God's kids, also need our most diligent efforts to nurture and protect them against people and philosophies that seek to turn them away from God and His truth.

Finally, God gave Adam one clear rule. He was not to eat of the tree of the knowledge of good and evil. The consequence was death. The only kind of death that Adam might understand and the only kind of death that really mattered in paradise was separation from God. The perfect, restful, comforting, and fulfilling intimacy Adam enjoyed while fellowshipping with and serving God in Paradise would come to an abrupt end if He disobeyed the commandment to resist this tree and continue in submission to God's judgment and wisdom to reveal to him what was good and what was evil. We are reminded to follow the same commandment today, to accept God's definition of good and evil. We are to train our children to obey God's commandment too **(see Deuteronomy 6:7).**

Today's text teaches us to find rest in doing God's work, to guard our hearts and minds against the foolishness of the world and the attacks of our enemies, and to submit to what God declares to be good and avoid what he labels evil as we *grow up into Christ*. These truths call us to be diligent to ensure that our children discover and grasp these truths too. Surely, today's public schools do not offer our children, God's kids, the blessings of His...

Rest, Responsibility, and Rule of Paradise.

Eden's First Lesson

"Then the Lord God said, 'It is not good that the man should be alone; I will make him a helper fit for him.' Now out of the ground the Lord God had formed every beast of the field and every bird of the heavens and brought them to the man to see what he would call them. And whatever the man called every living creature, that was its name. The man gave names to all livestock and to the birds of the heavens and to every beast of the field. But for Adam there was not found a helper fit for him" (Genesis 2:18-20).

Some important truths about God's relationship with humankind are revealed here. Here in the first classroom (Eden), God is the first teacher and Adam is the first student. The important lesson for Adam to learn is that *it is not good that the man should be alone.* If we look closely we will discover important truth about the way God has made us to learn.

Today's text teaches us that in the learning process, God reveals truth. This is an important truth for Christian learners. The record here shows that Adam did not discover the truth that he was alone simply by studying creation and naming the animals. Nor did he learn that being alone was not good, on his own. God spoke, and directly revealed that Adam was alone, adding His judgment that it was not good. We human beings are made to learn with the help of our Creator. God has given us His **"Spirit of Truth"** who, **"will guide you into all the truth"** (John 16:13).

If we believe that God created everything, then we must also believe that His truth is in everything. God's truth does not have to be integrated into our study of His world; it is already there, waiting to be revealed by **His Spirit of Truth.** Real truth seekers trust the Holy Spirit to reveal God's truth as they study God's creation. Great Christian truth seekers like Newton, Galileo, Kepler, Bacon, and others did not believe they discovered anything. Rather, they believed that God revealed truth as they studied His world around them.

This is the kind of education our children, God's kids deserve. Christian teachers who depend on the Holy Spirit in their lesson planning and in their classroom teaching will help students discover God's truth. Learning without guidance from God's *Spirit of Truth* and His revelation makes students vulnerable to deception and lies. God's kids deserve better, they deserve to learn from Godly teachers, filled with His Spirit, the first teacher who taught Adam, the first student...

Eden's First Lesson.

The First Wedding

"So the Lord God caused a deep sleep to fall upon the man, and while he slept took one of his ribs and closed up its place with flesh. And the rib that the Lord God had taken from the man he made into a woman and brought her to the man. Then the man said, 'This at last is bone of my bones and flesh of my flesh; she shall be called Woman, because she was taken out of Man.' Therefore a man shall leave his father and his mother and hold fast to his wife, and they shall become one flesh. And the man and his wife were both naked and were not ashamed" (Genesis 2:21-25).

Eden was fully prepared for a most wonderful event. God carefully planned and personally officiated the very first wedding! God created man alone so He could show His wisdom and care by creating a helper for him. If we look closely at today's text we see God's truth about marriage, the foundation of the family, and God's plan for us to trust that He knows and will meet all of our needs every day.

God created the woman from the man's rib to show the oneness He intended for them. He did not create the woman from the man's head lest he should rule over her. He did not create the woman from the man's feet lest he should trample on her. God used the man's rib to show that He wanted them to be very close to each other's heart and to be side-by-side in a protecting and caring way through life.

God created the man and the woman very different from each other. They would grow to appreciate their differences and learn to overcome the challenges these differences presented by loving each other and staying close to their Creator. They would learn how their differences complimented them together, enabled them to build a marriage, and become a family that would produce Godly offspring for the Lord.

We are surrounded today by the terrible consequences of not trusting the truths about marriage that God presents here. Failure to pursue and grasp God's truths about marriage has resulted in divorce, abuse, and multi-generational dysfunction on a large scale. Rebellion and rejection of these truths have led to homosexuality and much more disease and dysfunction. But the home becomes a wonderful place where spiritually healthy parents and children joyfully *grow up into Christ* together, when believers grasp and earnestly pursue the truths revealed by...

The First Wedding

Rising Up from the Fall

"Now the serpent was more crafty than any other beast of the field that the Lord God had made. He said to the woman, 'Did God actually say, "You shall not eat of any tree in the garden"?' And the woman said to the serpent, 'We may eat of the fruit of the trees in the garden, but God said, "You shall not eat of the fruit of the tree that is in the midst of the garden, neither shall you touch it, lest you die."' But the serpent said to the woman, 'You will not surely die. For God knows that when you eat of it your eyes will be opened, and you will be like God, knowing good and evil.' So when the woman saw that the tree was good for food, and that it was a delight to the eyes, and that the tree was to be desired to make one wise, she took of its fruit and ate, and she also gave some to her husband who was with her, and he ate" **(Genesis 3:6).**

Today's text shouts about the importance of holding fast to God's truth. The father of lies is introduced here and his strategy is exposed. At the same time, the path to victory over Satan and his schemes is revealed to genuine truth seekers.

The serpent was not wiser than Eve. The serpent **was more crafty than any other beast of the field,** but God granted mankind dominion over the animals. Adam and Eve had the advantage of knowing truth here that the serpent did not know. God had revealed His truth about the tree of the knowledge of good and evil to Adam and we see here that he had shared this truth with Eve. Note how the serpent needed Eve to tell him the truth that made this tree so different from all the others.

The serpent appealed to pride. He could not deny the truth, but he used pride to get Eve to submit to a corrupted version of the truth. He deceived Eve into believing that being like God would be better that submitting to God, then he deceived her into believing that the fruit of the tree was a way to become like God. In short, the serpent corrupted God's truth in order to break mankind's fellowship with God.

Satan is not a creator, he is a corrupter. Jesus called him the *"father of lies"* **(see John 8:44)**, or the corrupter of truth. He uses lies to keep people from seeking a relationship with God and to turn believers away from fellowship with God. This is why seeking and holding onto God's truth remains so vital today. This is why our children, God's kids, must be immersed in God's truth as much as possible, especially wherever and whenever they are being educated about God's world. The best defense against the schemes of the father of lies is to *"know the truth, and the truth will set you free"* **(John 8:32).**

Notice too, that because pride is the path away from God, humility is the way back to Him. *"If you confess with your mouth that Jesus is Lord and believe in your heart that God raised him from the dead, you will be saved"* **(Romans 10:9)**. It is through finding and submitting to the truth about Jesus Christ, Lord and Savior, that we are set free from deception, given victory over the father of lies, and restored to fellowship with our true Father. As you and your loved ones *grow up into Christ,* may you grow in your knowledge and understanding of God's truth, the path to victory over the father of lies. Truly, God's freedom giving is the path to...

Rising Up from the Fall.

The Blindness of Eden

"Then the eyes of both were opened, and they knew that they were naked. And they sewed fig leaves together and made themselves loincloths. And they heard the sound of the Lord God walking in the garden in the cool of the day, and the man and his wife hid themselves from the presence of the Lord God among the trees of the garden" (Genesis 3:7-8).

Why do bad things happen? Why is there so much evil in the world? The answer to these questions is revealed right here in the record of the consequences that immediately followed the first sin. Truth seekers will catch this one quickly. We lost our spiritual sight because of the fall in Eden.

The truth is that one immediate consequence of the fall was that Adam and Eve lost the ability to see good and evil as God did. They knew they were naked, but they had been naked all along. Their circumstance had not changed, but suddenly they saw their nakedness as shameful. God had created and declared them to be very good in their naked estate. Now they found their nakedness something to be scorned and they set about to try to correct the situation on their own.

An even more serious truth arises here. They hid themselves from God. How distorted their understanding had become! After their sin they believed that they were no longer loved and adored by their Creator. It is very noteworthy that they still had an awareness of the holiness of God, but now His holiness struck enough fear and shame in their hearts that it drove them from His presence.

Since Jesus Christ has paid the price for our sin and restored us to fellowship with God, we look forward to the restoration of Paradise in eternity. In the meantime, while we live in the flesh here in this fallen world, we continue to face temptation every day. But now we have the Holy Spirit in our hearts to restore our spiritual sight and to obey God every day. As we grow up into Christ, may God's Word and Spirit strengthen our spirits and give us victory over...

The Blindness of Eden.

When God Asks

"But the Lord God called to the man and said to him, 'Where are you?' And he said, 'I heard the sound of you in the garden, and I was afraid, because I was naked, and I hid myself.' He said, 'Who told you that you were naked? Have you eaten of the tree of which I commanded you not to eat?' The man said, 'The woman whom you gave to be with me, she gave me fruit of the tree, and I ate.' Then the Lord God said to the woman, 'What is this that you have done?' The woman said, 'The serpent deceived me, and I ate.'" (Genesis 3:9-13).

We find much soul-shaping truth here in Moses' record of God's reaction to the fall of Adam and Eve. There were many different ways God could have reacted to the first sin. He could have ended the lives of the first sinners immediately. He could have replaced Adam and Eve with another pair of humans in the hope that they would not disobey. But God came, calling, and asking some penetrating questions, and the future for Adam and Eve laid in how they answered when God asked.

God asked Adam, *"Where are you?"* God knew the obvious answer. He knew the reason for the answer. His question for Adam reveals the truth that Adam himself *did not know where he was*. He was not aware of the brokenness of his fellowship with God. The correct answer for Adam would have been, "I have sinned and I am now far from You. Please have mercy on me." The following questions God asked were to provoke awareness of the steps that led to his fall and repentance, or change of heart and mind, so he would not repeat the sin. The correct answers would have been something like, "I listened to and followed the deception of my wife and the serpent instead of obeying Your Word." Instead, Adam implied that God was to blame because He gave Adam the woman.

God still comes seeking and asking questions through His Word today. As we read the Bible and listen to His Word, God might ask us today, "Where have you been?" "What are you doing?" "Why are you doing that?" "Who are you listening to?" "Why won't you trust and obey me?"

45

Our future can be determined by our answers to God's questions every day. Our soul (heart, mind, and will) is shaped by our response to the probing questions presented through God's Word. And of course, our ultimate destiny is decided by our answer to God's big question, *"Where are you?"* The best answer ever spoken, one that has been spoken countless times throughout history remains, *"God, be merciful to me, a sinner!"* **(Luke 18:13).** As you and your family *grow up into Christ* may you learn to listen closely and answer...

When God Asks.

Victory over Temptation Revealed in the Serpent's Curse

"The Lord God said to the serpent, 'Because you have done this, cursed are you above all livestock and above all beasts of the field; on your belly you shall go, and dust you shall eat all the days of your life. I will put enmity between you and the woman, and between your offspring and her offspring; he shall bruise your head, and you shall bruise his heel.'" (Genesis 3:14-15).

There is important truth about the devil revealed here in the curse that God pronounced over the serpent that deceived the woman in the garden. God's Word clearly identifies the serpent mentioned here as the devil, *"And the great dragon was thrown down, that ancient serpent, who is called the devil and Satan, the deceiver of the whole world"* (Revelation 12:9). In today's text, truth seekers will find truth that gives freedom and victory over Satan.

The first truth is that just as the serpent has been completely transformed by the curse, so Satan has been changed by the curse. The serpent was attractive to Eve before the curse. After the curse, the serpent was condemned to slither along on the ground, far below all the rest of God's creatures. This truth is echoed in John's first epistle, *"Little children, you are from God and have overcome them, for he who is in you is greater than he who is in the world"* (1 John 4:4). Armed with this truth, believers can be assured of victory whenever we resist Satan and his temptations.

The second truth is that just as the serpent was condemned to eat dust for the rest of his life, Satan's influence over mankind has been reduced to that part of human beings that is made of the dust, or our flesh. Satan has no power over our soul or spirit, only our sinful nature. This truth is echoed in Matthew's gospel, *"Do not fear those who kill the body but cannot kill the soul. Rather fear him who can destroy both soul and body in hell"* (Matthew 10:28). Armed with this truth, believers who are filled

47

with the Holy Spirit and with the truth from God's Word will defeat Satan at every temptation.

The third truth is that just as the serpent's head will be crushed, so too the devil's head will be crushed by one born from the woman. To bruise the heel is to cripple or handicap someone. To crush the head is to completely destroy someone. Jesus Christ, conceived by the Holy Spirit and born of a woman, fulfilled this prophecy by destroying all the deception of the devil through His death and resurrection. This truth is echoed in John's first epistle, *"Whoever makes a practice of sinning is of the devil, for the devil has been sinning from the beginning. The reason the Son of God appeared was to destroy the works of the devil"* **(John 3:8).** Armed with this truth, believers can choose Christ's side in any battle brought on by temptation and experience victory over Satan because he is already defeated.

Of course, experiencing victory over Satan requires knowing and trusting truths like these that are revealed in God's Word. That's why it's so essential that we study God's Word every day and we equip our children, God's kids, with an education that is immersed in and supported by Biblical truth. As you and your children *grow up into Christ* may you discover and grasp God's truth, the key to...

Victory over Temptation Revealed in the Serpent's Curse.

Sin's Consequences and God's Discipline

"To the woman he said, 'I will surely multiply your pain in childbearing; in pain you shall bring forth children. Your desire shall be for your husband, and he shall rule over you.' And to Adam he said, 'Because you have listened to the voice of your wife and have eaten of the tree of which I commanded you, You shall not eat of it, cursed is the ground because of you; in pain you shall eat of it all the days of your life; thorns and thistles it shall bring forth for you; and you shall eat the plants of the field. By the sweat of your face you shall eat bread, till you return to the ground, for out of it you were taken; for you are dust, and to dust you shall return'" **(Genesis 3:16-19).**

Basic Christian truth is revealed in Moses' record of Adam and Eve's punishment. There is truth about what sets Christianity apart from other religions as well as truth about God's discipline here to be grasped by truth seekers.

God revealed His heart in the way He disciplined Adam and Eve. He did not curse them like He cursed the serpent. He did not change their shape and foretell their ultimate destruction. Instead His discipline of the first couple was all about relationship. God established a new order in their relationship with each other and with Him.

Now there would be submission and government in their relationship. Eve's devotion and submission to Adam would encourage her to trust his leadership. Adam's responsibility to lead and provide direction to Eve would motivate him to make attention and care to the family his priority. The resistance of the ground to their efforts to cultivate it would compel Adam and Eve to look to God for provision and direction.

The truth here is that God's discipline was designed to draw Adam and Eve closer together and closer to Him. His immediate reaction to the consequences of the first sin was to provide and encourage restoration of their broken relationships. The truth about Christianity is that it's all about relationship. Even sin's most obvious consequence, death, is designed to cause us to look to God, the Author of Life, for help in overcoming this most serious consequence of sin. And when we do seek Him, we meet the God *"who being found in human form, he humbled himself by becoming obedient to the point of death, even death on a cross"* **(Philippians 2:8).**

We still suffer and deal with the consequences of the first sin. This means we still enjoy the blessings of God's loving discipline which His Word promises will *"yield the peaceful fruit of righteousness to those who have been trained by it"* **(Hebrews 12:11).** As we continue to grow up into Christ, may we be drawn ever closer to our Father by...

Sin's Consequences and God's Discipline.

Clothed in His Righteousness

"The man called his wife's name Eve, because she was the mother of all living. And the Lord God made for Adam and for his wife garments of skins and clothed them" **(Genesis 3:20-21).**

When God clothed Adam and Eve with garments of skin, He was proclaiming two important truths about sin. Truth seekers will find encouragement here for victory over sin.

First, skins came from animals and represented the natural world. When God clothed Adam and Eve in animals' skins, He provided a reminder that they had renounced their spiritual lives in the first sin and were now consumed with life in the flesh. They would have to deal with all the frailties of life in a mortal body. Aging, disease, and more would consume their energies and attention and compete with God and heavenly things for their attention. But, by providing clothing for Adam and Eve, God revealed that He will always be near them and He would provide for their needs as they lived in this mortal world.

Second, animals had to die to provide their skins for Adam and Eve's clothing. This was a reminder that the consequence of sin was death. The depth of this truth is emphasized here because innocent animals were sacrificed to cover the consequence of sin for Adam and Eve. In killing animals to provide clothing for Adam and Eve, God revealed that He was willing to pay the terrible cost of their sin.

In all of this, God was purposefully illustrating the terrible truths about sin. At the same time, God was revealing two precious, encouraging truths about Himself. First, He will always be present with mankind as he struggles to deal with and overcome the consequences of sin in this life. Second, He will one day provide final atonement for sin, a final and decisive sacrifice and victory over sin for mankind. Then He will clothe believers, as members of His Church *"in fine linen, clean and white: for the fine linen is the righteousness of saints"* **(Revelation 19:8).** As we *grow up into Christ,* may we be thankful for the blood of Jesus that prepares us as His bride to spend eternity with Christ, where we'll be...

Clothed in His Righteousness.

Back to the Tree of Life

"Then the Lord God said, "Behold, the man has become like one of us in knowing good and evil. Now, lest he reach out his hand and take also of the tree of life and eat, and live forever—" therefore the Lord God sent him out from the garden of Eden to work the ground from which he was taken. He drove out the man, and at the east of the garden of Eden he placed the cherubim and a flaming sword that turned every way to guard the way to the tree of life" (Genesis 3:22-24).

Truth seekers must dig a little deep to discover and understand the truth behind God's banishment of Adam and Eve from the Tree of Life and the Garden of Eden. Skimming the surface here has produced confusion and misunderstanding. If we seek only the natural meaning we will miss the spiritual truth the Holy Spirit reveals here.

The first truth is that Adam and Eve had indeed become like one of the Trinity. The problem with that is they had become like God only in *"knowing good and evil"*. The whole truth is that knowing good and evil is not enough. Choosing to pursue and do that which is good makes man more like his Creator. Adam and Eve had already demonstrated that though they knew right from wrong, they did not obey. The results of disobedience were disastrous, with the loss of fellowship with God at the top of the list of serious consequences.

The next truth is directly related to the first. On the surface, it sounds good for Adam and Eve to live forever. However, God knows that after the fall this would be very bad. Adam and Eve's lives were filled with toil, hardship, pain, disease, and more as a result of the fall. To allow them to live forever in such a state would not be a blessing; rather it would be a terrible curse.

The truth is that in His mercy, God drove Adam and Eve from Eden. In placing the cherubim as a guard He implied that the Tree of Life would live on and be available again one day. God will nurture and care for the tree and in His timing and under His authority He will make a way back to the

Tree of Life one day. He tells us in His Word, *"Blessed are those who wash their robes, so that they may have the right to the tree of life and that they may enter the city by the gates"* (Revelation 22:14). As we *grow up into Christ,* we can trust God's promise that those who come to the Savior will find forgiveness and will be welcomed joyfully...

Back to the Tree of Life.

Victory Over Sin

"Now Adam knew Eve his wife, and she conceived and bore Cain, saying, 'I have gotten a man with the help of the Lord.' And again, she bore his brother Abel. Now Abel was a keeper of sheep, and Cain a worker of the ground. In the course of time Cain brought to the Lord an offering of the fruit of the ground, and Abel also brought of the firstborn of his flock and of their fat portions. And the Lord had regard for Abel and his offering, but for Cain and his offering he had no regard. So Cain was very angry, and his face fell. The Lord said to Cain, 'Why are you angry, and why has your face fallen? If you do well, will you not be accepted? And if you do not do well, sin is crouching at the door. Its desire is for you, but you must rule over it'" (Genesis 4:1-7).

Cain and Abel brought offerings to the Lord. We do not know if the concept of presenting offerings was something God taught the first family, or if this was simply the promptings of their hearts to connect with God. We do know that God said that the consequence of sin is death. He began here with the first family, to prepare mankind to look forward to the Savior who would atone for sin through His own sacrificial death. The reason why God accepted Abel's offering of the firstborn of his flock is made clear in the shadow of the cross.

Another important truth is revealed in today's text. Both Cain and Abel learned here that God accepts a particular kind of offering. God even spoke with Cain and told him that if he presented the right offering, he would be accepted too. God was teaching Cain the definition of sin. He showed Cain that sin is simply disobeying Him. God warned Cain that if he chose not to obey, temptation would gain control over him and lead him to commit serious sin. If he chose to obey he could rule over sin.

The truth is that if we spend time daily with the Lord in His Word, He will teach us daily what is right and wrong. He will bless us when we obey Him and He will correct us when we disobey Him. His never-changing truth remains... When we obey God, He will give us victory over sin. As we *grow up into Christ,* seeking to trust and obey Him every day, He will help us recognize and resist temptation, and He will grant us...

Victory Over Sin.

God's Tough Questions

"Cain spoke to Abel his brother. And when they were in the field, Cain rose up against his brother Abel and killed him. Then the Lord said to Cain, 'Where is Abel your brother?' He said, 'I do not know; am I my brother's keeper?' And the Lord said, 'What have you done? The voice of your brother's blood is crying to me from the ground. And now you are cursed from the ground, which has opened its mouth to receive your brother's blood from your hand. When you work the ground, it shall no longer yield to you its strength. You shall be a fugitive and a wanderer on the earth.' Cain said to the Lord, 'My punishment is greater than I can bear. Behold, you have driven me today away from the ground, and from your face I shall be hidden. I shall be a fugitive and a wanderer on the earth, and whoever finds me will kill me.' Then the Lord said to him, 'Not so! If anyone kills Cain, vengeance shall be taken on him sevenfold.' And the Lord put a mark on Cain, lest any who found him should attack him" (Genesis 4:8-15).

Today's text reveals truth about the devastating results of sin. Cain rejected the counsel of God to present an acceptable offering, whereupon God promised that he would conquer temptation and sin. Cain refused to change his thinking, to repent. As a result, sin conquered him. He was now a slave to sin. Jesus, the living Word, taught, *"Everyone who commits sin is a slave to sin"* (John 8:34).

The consequences of Cain's sin impacted many others. Abel's life was ended. Adam and Eve lost two sons. The family was now split in two. Augustine would see in this event the establishment of two cities among mankind, one godly and the other carnal. Cain's sin would infect and be remembered for generations, even being repeated with greater intensity by his great, great, great, grandson Lamech.

Truth seekers will find good news in the midst of this terrible sin story as once again, God came asking questions. When God asked Cain, *"Where is your brother?"* He was inviting Cain to confess his sin. When God asked, *"What have you done?"* He was inviting Cain to admit that he had rejected God's counsel, yielded to temptation, and was conquered by sin. Just as it was when God questioned his parents after the original sin, the direction of Cain's life after this sin depended on his answer to God's question. He responded with a lie and like his parents, he blamed God. A simple *"God, be merciful to me, a sinner"* **(Luke 18:13)** would have made all the difference.

The truth is that God is always asking us tough questions in order to restore our relationship and to draw us into intimate fellowship with Him. That's why we should make priority time with God, listening to His Word every day, especially when we've sinned. That's also why we should ensure that our children are immersed in God's Word while their worldview is being formed during school-aged years. As you and your family *grow up into Christ* may you hear from God through His Word every day, and may you be drawn ever closer to Him by your answers to...

God's Tough Questions.

Two Cities

"Then Cain went away from the presence of the Lord and settled in the land of Nod, east of Eden. Cain knew his wife, and she conceived and bore Enoch. When he built a city, he called the name of the city after the name of his son, Enoch. To Enoch was born Irad, and Irad fathered Mehujael, and Mehujael fathered Methushael, and Methushael fathered Lamech. And Lamech took two wives. The name of the one was Adah, and the name of the other Zillah. Adah bore Jabal; he was the father of those who dwell in tents and have livestock. His brother's name was Jubal; he was the father of all those who play the lyre and pipe. Zillah also bore Tubal-cain; he was the forger of all instruments of bronze and iron. The sister of Tubal-cain was Naamah" **(Genesis 4:16-22).**

Today's text raises a difficult question and reveals a significant truth. Because Jesus Christ said, ***"Your Word is truth"*** **(John 17:17),** genuine truth seekers who look to God's Word will find both answers to difficult questions and truth.

The obvious question is, where did Cain find a wife? Thus far, Moses has provided no record of the birth of a woman. However, because God's Word has called Eve, ***"the mother of all living"*** **(Genesis 3:20),** Eve must have given birth to at least one girl who grew up to become the wife of Cain. Why wasn't her birth mentioned in the record? Remember that sin had brought government to the family and God had made the man to be the leader and provider of the family. The Holy Spirit moved Moses to record only the births and names of significant men, and even fewer women in his writing.

The more subtle truth revealed in this text is that the first family was now forever divided into two groups. Moses records that Cain set about building a city and naming it after his son Enoch. This city represented a lineage that was born of flesh and consumed with earthly things. Because his life was cut short by the sin of his brother Cain, Abel had only been a pilgrim here on the earth and his home would be a city in heaven. Augustine identified the founding of two cities here representing the earthly and heavenly lives all human beings. Non-believers are born of the flesh and consumed by the cares of this earthly world. Believers are born of the Spirit and while sojourning here on earth should have their hearts and minds *"set on things above, not on things on the earth"* **(Colossians 3:2).**

As we *grow up into Christ,* may we become less consumed by earthly things and more compelled by heavenly things. As believers we are pilgrims and citizens of...

Two Cities.

God's Law Written on Our Hearts

"Lamech said to his wives:
'Adah and Zillah, hear my voice;
you wives of Lamech, listen to what I say:
I have killed a man for wounding me,
a young man for striking me.
If Cain's revenge is sevenfold,
then Lamech's is seventy-sevenfold.'" **(Genesis 4:23-24).**

Truth seekers will quickly notice the difference between Lamech's sin and the sins of Adam, Eve, and Cain. While the former sinners denied or shifted blame for their sins, Lamech was quick to confess his sin. Without any record of prompting, he declared his sin to his wives. (By the way, here is the first example of polygamy in the Bible. It comes in the line of Cain, those living in the earthly city where mankind's priorities are carnal, temporal things and pleasures. God's purpose for marriage and family from the very beginning was one man and one woman).

The truth revealed today is that we have a conscience that convicts us when we do wrong. We may have this gift because we are made in the image and after the likeness of God. Or we inherited it as a consequence of Adam and Eve eating of the tree of the knowledge of good and evil. Conscience's first appearance was when Adam and Eve were convicted that they were naked after they sinned. The truth is that like Lamech, we all have something inside us that convicts us when we sin. Through the apostle Paul the Holy Spirit teaches that, ***"The conscience is like a law written in the human heart. And it will show whether we are forgiven or condemned"*** **(Romans 2:15).**

Lamech's story reveals the truth that while everyone has a conscience; it's our response to the promptings of our conscience that matters. When Adam, Eve, and Cain sinned, God came, calling, and asking tough questions designed to prompt confession and repentance. When Lamech sinned, he responded to the prompting of his conscience, the law written on his heart, and he confessed immediately, even though there is evidence that his action was in self-defense. There is no record of God questioning or disciplining him.

As believers living in this rebellious world, we battle against temptation and sin every day. When we sin, our conscience will convict us to confess and repent so that we will overcome sin and continue to grow in our relationship and fellowship with the Lord. This is why God has provided a simple and clear way to forgiveness when we sin... *"If we confess our sins, he is faithful and just to forgive us our sins and to cleanse us from all unrighteousness"* **(1 John 1:9).** As *we grow up into Christ*, may we be quick to respond with confession and repentance to the promptings of our conscience,...

God's Law Written on Our Hearts.

Worthy of Our Trust and Devotion

"And Adam knew his wife again, and she bore a son and called his name Seth, for she said, 'God has appointed for me another offspring instead of Abel, for Cain killed him.' To Seth also a son was born, and he called his name Enosh. At that time people began to call upon the name of the Lord" (Genesis 4:25-26).

Two truths are revealed in today's scripture. God appointed a replacement for Abel and people began to call upon the name of the Lord.

The first truth is that God is faithful to keep His promises. He included Adam and Eve in the process of filling the earth with *"godly offspring"* (Malachi 2:15). His plan was not thwarted by Cain's sin. This truth is expressed in the words of Paul, *"All the promises of God find their Yes in him (Jesus Christ)"* (2 Corinthians 1:20). Christ followers can count on all of God's promises no matter what the surrounding circumstances imply.

The second truth is that God compels people to know Him intimately. Though we seem to drift away from Him, He is always there calling us back to intimacy with Him. Note that people began to call upon the name of *Yahweh* (Hebrew: *the Self-Existent, Eternal God Who Is*). This is the very personal Hebrew name for God. Jesus taught that this truth is to be our highest priority in life, *"This is eternal life, that they know you the only true God, and Jesus Christ whom you have sent"* (John 17:3). Here is a reminder and a call to truth seekers to be devoted to learning more about God in all of life. Here is a prompting for Christian parents to see that their children (God's kids) are learning about God and His truth as they are educated and prepared for life as adults. Here is the truth that eternal life is to be devoted to knowing our Father.

As you and your children (God's Kids) *grow up into Christ,* may you find His promises sure and may you be able to say you know Him better every day. He truly is...

Worthy of Our Trust and Devotion.

God Rewards Those Who Seek Him

"This is the book of the generations of Adam. When God created man, he made him in the likeness of God. Male and female he created them, and he blessed them and named them Man when they were created. When Adam had lived 130 years, he fathered a son in his own likeness, after his image, and named him Seth. The days of Adam after he fathered Seth were 800 years; and he had other sons and daughters. Thus all the days that Adam lived were 930 years, and he died. When Seth had lived 105 years, he fathered Enosh. Seth lived after he fathered Enosh 807 years and had other sons and daughters. Thus all the days of Seth were 912 years, and he died" (Genesis 5:1-8).

Today's scripture reveals two truths about human nature and one victorious truth about Himself. If we believe the truth that God created Adam and Eve, the first humans, in *His image and after His likeness* **(see Genesis 1:26)** then these anthropological and theological truths rise to the surface in today's study. If we believe something else about the origin of mankind, we will miss the truth, and the results can be devastating and defeating for individuals as well as for humanity in general.

The first truth is revealed in the Holy Spirit's repeating that God made Adam in His likeness. This is a reminder that we have within us the image, or the shadow of our Creator. This image compels us to connect with our Creator, as evidenced by the record in the previous verse, *"At that time people began to call upon the name of the LORD"* **(Genesis 4:26).** We are made like Him to enjoy fellowship with Him.

The next truth is revealed in the words, Adam *"fathered a son in his own likeness, after his image"* **(verse 3).** Here, the Holy Spirit teaches that we have inherited the shadow, or sin nature of our father Adam. As children of Adam, we have within us the propensity to sin.

The obvious conclusion is that we have two competing natures within us. We have a desire to be intimate with God, but we also have a compulsion to have our own way and hide from Him. We are constantly confronted with a choice to be with our Father or to run away from Him. But there is a very important truth about God here that points the way to victory in this ongoing battle...

Note that the line of Cain, the family that represents the earthly city that was consumed with carnal and material things, began and ended with murder and death. However, the line of Abel, the family that represents the city that was built on a godly foundation and concerned with heavenly things, begins with God and is consumed with *"calling on the name of the LORD"*. From this point, we read no more about Cain's family, but the rest of history (God's story) is focused on the line descended from Seth. We learn here that God *"rewards those who seek Him"* (Hebrews 11:6).

The truth is, *as we grow up into Christ,* whenever we seek the Lord in the midst of the battle between the spirit and the flesh, God meets us and grants us victory, so we might be restored to sweet intimacy and fellowship with Him because...

God Rewards Those Who Seek Him.

The Sovereignty and Mercy of God

"When Enosh had lived 90 years, he fathered Kenan. Enosh lived after he fathered Kenan 815 years and had other sons and daughters. Thus all the days of Enosh were 905 years, and he died. When Kenan had lived 70 years, he fathered Mahalalel. Kenan lived after he fathered Mahalalel 840 years and had other sons and daughters. Thus all the days of Kenan were 910 years, and he died. When Mahalalel had lived 65 years, he fathered Jared. Mahalalel lived after he fathered Jared 830 years and had other sons and daughters. Thus all the days of Mahalalel were 895 years, and he died. When Jared had lived 162 years he fathered Enoch. Jared lived after he fathered Enoch 800 years and had other sons and daughters. Thus all the days of Jared were 962 years, and he died" **(Genesis 5:9-20).**

It's just a list of names. It's a simple genealogy. But, for the hungry truth-seeker, there is wonderful truth to be gained here because the Spirit of Truth moved Moses to record these words and place them here just for us to see, study, and grow on. There is very little information provided about each person in this list, only where they fall in the succession from Adam to Noah and how long they lived

Sometimes the Spirit reveals truth in what is included in God's Word, but sometimes He reveals truth in what is excluded. In saying nothing about the personalities, character, or achievements of the men in this genealogy, God is making the point that He does not choose people to be a part of His plans based upon some sort of merit or personal worth that they might possess. The names of these select men are listed forever in God's Word simply because God chose them. This reflects an important truth, the sovereignty of God. The Spirit repeats this truth through Paul, *"He has mercy on whomever he wills, and he hardens whomever he wills"* **(Romans 9:18).**

Another truth is revealed in the longevity of the men in this genealogy. While their long lives may be the result of living in a pollution-free, near perfect world, the real truth is that they spent long years living under the curse that resulted from the first sin. These men lived nearly a thousand years in a struggle to survive, battling nature that resisted their efforts to farm and provide for their families, watching their women endure the pain of childbearing, and so much more. In His mercy, God would one day shorten the sentence of this mortal life to 120 years **(see Genesis 6:3).** Both the sovereignty and the mercy of God are revealed in the number of days, months, and years people spend here on earth.

As we live out our lives here on earth, preparing for the real, eternal life to come, our perspective about life should be maturing. We should be trusting God's sovereignty and appreciating His mercy more and more as we learn from the truth He reveals to us in His Word. As we *grow up into Christ,* we are truly blessed by...

The Sovereignty and Mercy of God.

The Blessings of Walking with God

"When Enoch had lived 65 years, he fathered Methuselah. Enoch walked with God after he fathered Methuselah 300 years and had other sons and daughters. Thus all the days of Enoch were 365 years. Enoch walked with God, and he was not, for God took him. When Methuselah had lived 187 years, he fathered Lamech. Methuselah lived after he fathered Lamech 782 years and had other sons and daughters. Thus all the days of Methuselah were 969 years, and he died" **(Genesis 5:21-27).**

Today we learn two very practical truths from one of the most profound events of the earliest days, the translation of Enoch to a life so close to God that here on earth, he was no more! Truth is revealed in the answers to two questions...

What does it mean to *walk with God?* The Holy Spirit answers this question in two places. First, Enoch lived a faith-filled life and sought to please God. *"By faith Enoch was taken up so that he should not see death, and he was not found, because God had taken him. Now before he was taken he was commended as having pleased God"* **(Hebrews 11:5).** Second, Enoch prophesied (foretold, spoke under inspiration), to his generation. *"It was also about these that Enoch, the seventh from Adam, prophesied, saying, 'Behold, the Lord comes with ten thousands of his holy ones, to execute judgment on all and to convict all the ungodly of all their deeds of ungodliness that they have committed in such an ungodly way, and of all the harsh things that ungodly sinners have spoken against him'"* **(Jude 1:14-15).** The Holy Spirit defines *walking with God* here as living so close to God so as to trust in Him above all else, and to proclaim to others what God reveals in our intimate fellowship with Him. For all truth seekers, this means spending time with God listening to and responding to His Word, then courageously sharing His truth with others in word and deed. We need Christian schools that encourage our children to *walk with God* by immersing them in God's truth from the earliest age possible.

Why should believers strive to *walk with God?* The blessings of Enoch's *walk with God* are available to anyone who follows his example. His intimacy with God empowered Enoch to live above the consequences of temptation and sin of this world, and to be a prophet to his and succeeding generations. Then, God took Enoch out of this cursed world, to walk closely with Him forever. As we *grow up into Christ,* may we, like Enoch, experience...

The Blessings of Walking with God.

How Do You Spell R-E-L-I-E-F?

"When Lamech had lived 182 years, he fathered a son and called his name Noah, saying, 'Out of the ground that the Lord has cursed, this one shall bring us relief from our work and from the painful toil of our hands.' Lamech lived after he fathered Noah 595 years and had other sons and daughters. Thus all the days of Lamech were 777 years, and he died. After Noah was 500 years old, Noah fathered Shem, Ham, and Japheth" **(Genesis 5:28-32).**

On occasion in the 1970s, when schoolchildren were asked to spell the word "relief", they would respond with "Rolaids", the result of a very successful advertising campaign that asked, *"How do you spell relief? - R-O-L-A-I-D-S"* In today's text, men and women living long under the curse and consequences of sin sought relief. Through the example of Enoch, God had shown that the way to relief was to walk closely with Him. But it seemed no one got the message. So God raised up another man, Noah, who like Enoch, *"walked with God"* **(Genesis 6:9).** Through Noah, some powerful truths about God's providence and mercy are revealed for truth seekers to hold onto.

First, note that Noah had no children until he was 500 years old **(Genesis 5:32 and 6:10 confirm this).** Can you imagine what might be going through the minds and hearts of Noah and his wife as they had no children during this time when everyone else around them was so fruitful? They did not see or understand God's plan to deliver them and the young families of their sons from the corruption of this world in order to start a new one in the future. But, through it all, *"Noah was a righteous man, blameless in his generation. Noah walked with God"* **(Genesis 6:9).** Noah trusted the great plan and providence of God.

Lamech's prophecy about Noah and his name also reveal the truth that God is merciful. When He delivered Enoch from this sin cursed world, God was rewarding Enoch for faithfully walking with Him. But, through Noah, God would deliver all of undeserving mankind, those who had been far from God, from their *"work and from the painful toil of our hands".* God

70

defines His mercy here by offering sinners *"relief"*, which is something they do not deserve. Before the flood, God reached out to sinners through Noah, *"who preached about being right with God"* (2 Peter 2:5, NCV). In His great mercy He allowed them nearly 1,000 (one of God's numbers for perfection) years to repent. Then He ended their trials and relieved their burden through the flood. Those who responded to Noah's preaching found forgiveness and more; eternal relief (more on gospel truth revealed in Noah's message coming soon).

As we *grow up into Christ* in this sin cursed world, may our trust in God's great plan and our confidence in God's great mercy provoke others to ask us...

How Do You Spell R-E-L-I-E-F?

Truth About gods and the Gospel Revealed in Genesis

"When man began to multiply on the face of the land and daughters were born to them, the sons of God saw that the daughters of man were attractive. And they took as their wives any they chose. Then the Lord said, 'My Spirit shall not abide in man forever, for he is flesh: his days shall be 120 years.' The Nephilim were on the earth in those days, and also afterward, when the sons of God came in to the daughters of man and they bore children to them. These were the mighty men who were of old, the men of renown" **(Genesis 6:1-4).**

Moses records that angels forsook the eternal beauty of God and heaven for the temporal, mortal beauty of the women of earth. They produced children by human women who grew up to become *"mighty men who were of old, the men of renown".* When we study history we discover that every culture has a record of giants and mythological heroes. Because they rejected God's truth, people often called and worshipped these "super humans" as *gods and goddesses.* However, when we study history in the light of God's Word, we discover the truth about these figures. They are the fallen angels and their offspring identified by the Spirit of Truth here in Genesis. To help our children (God's kids) discern the difference between false gods and the One True God today, it is imperative that we follow God's command... *"These words that I command you today shall be on your heart. You shall teach them diligently to your children, and shall talk of them when you sit in your house, and when you walk by the way, and when you lie down, and when you rise"* **(Deuteronomy 6:6-7).** God wants our children (His kids) to learn His truth as they study His world, and education that is built on the truth of His Word is the best way to instill His truth in their hearts.

In the middle of this important history lesson, Moses interjects God's decision to reduce the longevity of human beings to 120 years. Once again, God demonstrates His mercy in reducing the suffering of this mortal life while still allowing 120 years for men and women to discover

His truth, repent, and receive forgiveness. Through Abel's sacrifice, Enoch's rapture, and Noah's preaching, God had revealed the basic truths of the gospel. We are separated from God by sin. We need a sacrifice to atone for sin. When we obey God by accepting His sacrifice, we are forgiven. The gospel truth revealed here in Genesis points clearly to Jesus Christ, who fulfilled every bit of it at Calvary.

As we grow up into Christ, may we be ever mindful and thankful for the...

Truth About gods and the Gospel Revealed in Genesis.

Grieved Him to His Heart

"The Lord saw that the wickedness of man was great in the earth, and that every intention of the thoughts of his heart was only evil continually. And the Lord regretted that he had made man on the earth, and it grieved him to his heart. So the Lord said, 'I will blot out man whom I have created from the face of the land, man and animals and creeping things and birds of the heavens, for I am sorry that I have made them' (Genesis 6:5-7).

To discover the truth in today's scripture we must look closely at the original language, Hebrew. Our Teacher, the Spirit of Truth, intentional chose this language and these words to compel us to seek and grasp God's truth. Moses records here that God saw and judged the hearts of mankind. He declared that *"every intention of the thoughts of his heart was only evil continually"*. There are three key words here that reveal the truth about the hearts of human beings.

Intention - Hebrew: *yēṣer; imagination, frame, conception.*

Thoughts - Hebrew: *maḥashābâ; contrivance, plan, cunning, purpose.*

Heart - Hebrew: *lēb; heart, mind, understanding, feelings, will.*

Taken together, these three words define something unique about human beings. Because we're created in God's image, He placed within us the ability to reason. Above all other creatures, we can perceive, consider, and reason about our world, ourselves, and our Creator. Taken together, our imaginations, sense of purpose, and understanding form our worldview, which is the way we see and respond to our world.

God made us this way so we can be shaped by seeking and discovering His truth. When we seek and grasp His truth we come closer to God. He made us for close, intimate fellowship with Him. So far in Moses' record we see that God proclaimed His truth clearly in creation and through the lives of several righteous men (Abel, Seth, Enoch, and Noah). But the record also shows that mankind's rejection of God's truth was so wholesale that God's heart was filled with pity and grief over mankind, and He was about to act.

Today's truth compels us to reflect on our own worldview. What shapes our imagination and forms our conceptions of God's world? Is it truth or deception that forms our sense of purpose? Are our understanding, feeling, and will shaped by worldly foolishness or God's truth? Who and what is forming the worldview of our children (God's kids)? As we *grow up into Christ* may our Father be blessed to find us set apart from the world by His truth **(see John 17:17)** and not among those who...

Grieved Him to His Heart.

Find Favor in the Eyes of God

"But Noah found favor in the eyes of the Lord. These are the generations of Noah. Noah was a righteous man, blameless in his generation. Noah walked with God. And Noah had three sons, Shem, Ham, and Japheth" (Genesis 6:8-10).

Some days we have to dig deep to find the truth in God's Word. Other days, like today, His truth leaps off the pages at us. As we study and enjoy God's Word every day, we look to the Holy Spirit to reveal God's truth and implant it in our hearts and minds.

The big truth here is that while God saw so much wickedness in the hearts and minds of everyone around him He was moved to destroy mankind, Noah found favor in God's eyes. That's what I want, to find favor in the Father's eyes. What was different about Noah?

Noah was a righteous man. Noah accepted God's determination about what was right and what was wrong, what was good and what was evil. And Noah pursued God's righteousness. This set him apart from everyone else around him as they were pursuing their own selfish and wicked desires.

Noah walked with God. Like Enoch before him, Noah spent much time in the presence of God, listening to His voice and sharing life with Him. Unlike everyone else around him, fellowship with the Father was a priority for Noah.

Until Jesus returns, our world continues to be in rebellion against God. Everything and everyone around us tempts us to reject and ignore God. But, truth seekers love to discover and pursue God's righteousness and to walk closely with Him, two holy habits that set us apart from the rest of this world, help us to *grow up into Christ*, and promise that like Noah, we may...

Find Favor in the Eyes of God.

Hear and Obey God's Word

"Now the earth was corrupt in God's sight, and the earth was filled with violence. And God saw the earth, and behold, it was corrupt, for all flesh had corrupted their way on the earth. And God said to Noah, 'I have determined to make an end of all flesh, for the earth is filled with violence through them. Behold, I will destroy them with the earth. Make yourself an ark of gopher wood. Make rooms in the ark, and cover it inside and out with pitch. This is how you are to make it: the length of the ark 300 cubits, its breadth 50 cubits, and its height 30 cubits. Make a roof for the ark, and finish it to a cubit above, and set the door of the ark in its side. Make it with lower, second, and third decks'" **(Genesis 6:11-16).**

Because Noah found favor in the eyes of God (he pursued righteousness and he walked with God), he was available to God. The Lord knew that when He spoke, Noah would listen. He could hear God and he could be used by God because Noah knew how to trust and obey God. And did God ever use Noah in a very big way... God used Noah to preserve a remnant of the human race and to point the way to forgiveness and salvation for all truth seekers!

Because Noah sought God's righteousness, he was able to hear and accept God's Word, that He was about to *"make an end of all flesh"*. I'm sure this was difficult for Noah to hear and even harder to accept. Beyond his immediate family, all of his extended family, friends, neighbors, and all living human beings were going to be destroyed. Noah did not question why or how, but trusted that God had a plan and that His plan was good.

Because Noah walked with God, he was available to follow the Lord's instructions and build a way of escape for himself and his immediate family. Walking closely with God had already set Noah apart from the rest of the world. Living above the corruption and sin that encompassed him enabled Noah to believe and think differently than those around him. He was ready to follow God's instructions and begin building an enormous ark, something that had never been attempted before.

The truth is that God is still looking for truth seekers who are able to hear and obey Him today. Churches and Christian schools are preparing truth seekers like Noah to seek and follow God's leading today and tomorrow. As we *grow up into Christ* may we pursue God's righteousness and walk closely with Him so that like Noah, we too are able to do supernatural things when we...

Hear and Obey God's Word.

Living in the Covenant and Providence of God

"'For behold, I will bring a flood of waters upon the earth to destroy all flesh in which is the breath of life under heaven. Everything that is on the earth shall die. But I will establish my covenant with you, and you shall come into the ark, you, your sons, your wife, and your sons' wives with you. And of every living thing of all flesh, you shall bring two of every sort into the ark to keep them alive with you. They shall be male and female. Of the birds according to their kinds, and of the animals according to their kinds, of every creeping thing of the ground, according to its kind, two of every sort shall come in to you to keep them alive. Also take with you every sort of food that is eaten, and store it up. It shall serve as food for you and for them.' Noah did this; he did all that God commanded him" (Genesis 6:17-22).

Two encouraging truths are presented in today's scripture as God promises a covenant with Noah and his descendants and as God brings the animals to the ark.

First, we see that God proposes a covenant with Noah. God gave no details of the covenant, but with the words *"I will establish my covenant with you"* God promised a future covenant. The promise meant that Noah and his family would surely survive the destruction of the worldwide flood that was soon to come. Even before teaching Noah exactly what a covenant was, the key ingredients of a covenant were present. The condition required for Noah to receive the blessings of this covenant was obedience. If Noah obeyed God's Word, to build an ark and care for the animals that would fill it, he and his family would survive the flood and inherit the covenant.

Second, God promised that the animals *"shall come in to you"*. Noah would not have to go on a massive hunt. He would not have to select the perfect pair of each species. Can you imagine the difficulty of capturing animals as large as elephants and as small as fleas? God would take care of this enormous detail. Noah would simply trust God's providence.

Christ has established a new covenant with His followers through His blood... *"This cup that is poured out for you is the new covenant in my blood"* (Luke 22:20). Paul taught that Christ followers can trust in God's providence... *"My God will supply every need of yours according to his riches in glory in Christ Jesus"* (Philippians 4:19). As you *grow up into Christ,* may you and your loved ones experience the sure blessings and promises of God because you are...

Living in the Covenant and Providence of God.

Escape from a Stubborn World

'Then the Lord said to Noah, 'Go into the ark, you and all your household, for I have seen that you are righteous before me in this generation. Take with you seven pairs of all clean animals, the male and his mate, and a pair of the animals that are not clean, the male and his mate, and seven pairs of the birds of the heavens also, male and female, to keep their offspring alive on the face of all the earth. For in seven days I will send rain on the earth forty days and forty nights, and every living thing that I have made I will blot out from the face of the ground.' And Noah did all that the Lord had commanded him" (Genesis 7:1-5).

In the face of obvious miracles, people still refused to repent. God granted one hundred years while the ark was being made, and still that rebellious generation did not repent. God gathered beasts that they had never seen into the ark and still they did not repent. He established a state of peace between predator and prey and still they did not repent. God delayed seven more days after Noah and the animals entered the ark, leaving the great door of the ark wide open to them. No lion tried to return to its jungle home and no bird attempted escape to visit its familiar habitat. Although that generation saw all that went on inside and outside of the ark, they stubbornly refused to repent.

Peter recalled the disobedience of Noah's generation as an accurate description of those who stubbornly reject the obvious miracle of God's forgiveness displayed in the life, death, and resurrection of Jesus Christ... *"They formerly did not obey, when God's patience waited in the days of Noah, while the ark was being prepared"* (1 Peter 3:20). The Spirit of Truth reveals that God's patience and Noah's faithful obedience despite strong rejection resulted in salvation for anyone willing to repent and believe. God is still patient with mankind and we can still follow Noah's example of faithful obedience in the face of the stubborn rejection that we encounter. As we *grow up into Christ,* is spite of the disobedience and rejection we encounter, may we faithfully share His good news, the only...

Escape from a Stubborn World.

Truth that Saved Even the Animals

"Noah was six hundred years old when the flood of waters came upon the earth. And Noah and his sons and his wife and his sons' wives with him went into the ark to escape the waters of the flood. Of clean animals, and of animals that are not clean, and of birds, and of everything that creeps on the ground, two and two, male and female, went into the ark with Noah, as God had commanded Noah" (Genesis 7:6-9).

Two Biblical truths that are foundational to our worldview are presented in today's scripture. Truth seekers will find truth about creation and truth about mankind here. But if we ignore God's Word in our study of the living world (Biology) and mankind (Anthropology) we will miss God's truth. The consequences are devastating and eternal.

The Spirit of Truth reveals important truth in the record of every living animal coming into the ark along with Noah and his family. Why was God going to destroy the animals? They did not sin. Why did God summon them to the ark? He could have recreated them after the flood with a word, just as he had in the beginning **(See Genesis 1:20,22,24).** God was showing mankind the truth that because He created human beings to be stewards of His creatures **(see Genesis 1:26,28),** mankind's disobedience brought terrible consequences to all of creation. The Spirit moved Paul to echo this truth in his epistle to the Romans, *"For the creation was subjected to futility, not willingly, but because of him who subjected it"* **(Romans 8:20).**

The Spirit of Truth also teaches here that because Noah and his family obeyed God and entered the ark, the creatures submitted to their leadership and followed them into the ark, and all were saved from the flood. Again, the same Spirit leads truth seekers to this same truth through the pen of the apostle Paul, *"The creation itself will be set free from its bondage to corruption and obtain the freedom of the glory of the children of God"* **(Romans 8:21).**

When we study and believe the truth from God's Word, like Noah, we are saved from the consequences of sin and discover that we can bring blessings or consequences to God's world and His creatures. When our children are educated in the truth revealed in God's Word, as they *grow up into Christ,* they will learn the...

Truth that Saved Even the Animals.

God's Patience, Perfecting, and Protection

"And after seven days the waters of the flood came upon the earth. In the six hundredth year of Noah's life, in the second month, on the seventeenth day of the month, on that day all the fountains of the great deep burst forth, and the windows of the heavens were opened. And rain fell upon the earth forty days and forty nights. On the very same day Noah and his sons, Shem and Ham and Japheth, and Noah's wife and the three wives of his sons with them entered the ark, they and every beast, according to its kind, and all the livestock according to their kinds, and every creeping thing that creeps on the earth, according to its kind, and every bird, according to its kind, every winged creature. They went into the ark with Noah, two and two of all flesh in which there was the breath of life. And those that entered, male and female of all flesh, went in as God had commanded him. And the Lord shut him in" (Genesis 7:10-16).

There are several encouraging truths presented here.

First, the waters did not come until seven days after Noah entered the ark. The number seven is used 287 times in the Old Testament. In Hebrew the number seven signifies completion and perfection. The Lord's plan to destroy all flesh was not complete without a period of time for repentance. The seven days Noah, his family, and the enormous number of saved creatures spent waiting inside the ark revealed the perfect *patience* of the Lord as He gave mankind another opportunity to repent.

Then there is the forty day and night period of the rising flood waters. There are thirty-two significant uses of the number forty in the Bible. The number forty is used by God to represent a period of testing or judgment. While God was judging the earth for mankind's sin, He was also *perfecting* the faith and character of Noah and his family. The Lord was preparing Noah and his family for the great task ahead by testing and refining their faith. After all, God was counting on Noah and his family to repopulate the earth and bring the Messiah to mankind through Noah's descendants.

Finally, *"The Lord shut him in".* God provided *protection* for all life within the ark by closing the huge door and sealing every nook and cranny of this enormous ship. The indispensable truth revealed here is that when we trust and obey the Lord, He will protect us even as He is judging the evil around us. This truth is echoed by David... *"But you, O LORD, are a shield about me, my glory, and the lifter of my head"* **(Psalm 3:3),** and by Jesus Christ himself... *"I do not ask that you take them out of the world, but that you keep them from the evil one"* **(John 17:15).**

As we *grow up into Christ,* and we encounter the wickedness of the world around us, Noah's story reminds us that we can count on...

God's Patience, Perfecting, and Protection.

Choosing Life is as Simple as A, B, C

"The flood continued forty days on the earth. The waters increased and bore up the ark, and it rose high above the earth. The waters prevailed and increased greatly on the earth, and the ark floated on the face of the waters. And the waters prevailed so mightily on the earth that all the high mountains under the whole heaven were covered. The waters prevailed above the mountains, covering them fifteen cubits deep. And all flesh died that moved on the earth, birds, livestock, beasts, all swarming creatures that swarm on the earth, and all mankind. Everything on the dry land in whose nostrils was the breath of life died. He blotted out every living thing that was on the face of the ground, man and animals and creeping things and birds of the heavens. They were blotted out from the earth. Only Noah was left, and those who were with him in the ark. And the waters prevailed on the earth 150 days" **(Genesis 7:17-24).**

Sometimes truth is obvious. It can be as clear as the nose on our face. Because God wants us to choose wisely and receive His blessing, He has made the difference between good and evil as simple as A, B, C. In today's text, God sends 40 days and nights of rain that produce 150 days of destruction on earth that destroys every living thing, except Noah, *"A righteous man, blameless in his generation"* **(Genesis 6:9).** Here the Holy Spirit reveals three truths that compel us to choose God and His righteousness.

First, God loves righteousness and hates wickedness. *"You have loved righteousness and hated wickedness"* **(Psalm 45:7).** Second, God loves those who pursue righteousness and reject wickedness. *"The way of the wicked is an abomination to the LORD, but he loves him who pursues righteousness"* **(Proverbs 15:9).** Third, God preserves the righteous and judges the wicked. *"He did not spare the ancient world, but preserved Noah, a herald of righteousness, with seven others, when he brought a flood upon the world of the ungodly"* **(2 Peter 2:5).**

How do we choose righteousness? It's as clear and simple as A, B, C. Admit the truth about ourselves, that we are sinners who naturally choose wickedness. We have lots of company. The Bible reveals the truth about us... *"All have sinned and fall short of the glory of God"* **(Romans 3:23).**

Believe the truth about God, that He provided forgiveness through the sacrifice of His Son Jesus Christ. The Bible reveals the truth that Jesus Christ paid for our sin... *"He himself bore our sins in his body on the tree, that we might die to sin and live to righteousness"* **(1 Peter 2:24).**

Commit our trust to Jesus Christ as Savior and Lord. The Bible reveals the truth about the way to forgiveness and salvation... *"Believe in the Lord Jesus, and you will be saved"* **(Acts 16:31).**

Trusting God's simple truth about forgiveness and salvation is the first step to eternal life, where the presence and work of His Spirit helps us *grow up into Christ.* Noah's life reveals the truth that...

Choosing Life is as Simple as A, B, C.

But God Remembers

"But God remembered Noah and all the beasts and all the livestock that were with him in the ark. And God made a wind blow over the earth, and the waters subsided. The fountains of the deep and the windows of the heavens were closed, the rain from the heavens was restrained, and the waters receded from the earth continually. At the end of 150 days the waters had abated, and in the seventh month, on the seventeenth day of the month, the ark came to rest on the mountains of Ararat. And the waters continued to abate until the tenth month; in the tenth month, on the first day of the month, the tops of the mountains were seen" (Genesis 8:1-5).

Tossed about violently by wind and waves for 150 days, no end of rising waters in sight, food running low, the rickety ark straining to stay together, anxiety among both animals and people growing by the hour, these were the conditions Noah and his family endured around the clock. Yet, the Holy Spirit interjects a very encouraging word of truth with, *"But God remembered Noah"*.

The Hebrew word for remember means *to mark, to be mindful of, to think on.* Although external conditions pointed to the feeling that God had forgotten them, the truth was that God's mind was firmly fixed on Noah, his family, and all the life that was preserved in the ark. After all, this family was faithfully obeying God's Word and although it was very difficult, they were keeping themselves right in the center of His will.

Throughout His Word, God declares that He remembers individuals and nations. Often when Israel was experiencing its darkest moments, in exile or under attack, God's Word reveals that His mind was fixed on them. In other places, especially in the Book of Revelation, God is very mindful of the wickedness of individuals and the iniquity of governments like Babylon.

As we *grow up into Christ* here in this sinful world, it is inevitable that the storms, trials, and temptations of life will make us feel forgotten by

God from time to time. If we spend consistent time in His Word and strive to walk closely with Him, the Spirit of truth will remind us, especially in those tough times...

But God Remembers.

Ravens, Doves, and Serving God

"At the end of forty days Noah opened the window of the ark that he had made and sent forth a raven. It went to and fro until the waters were dried up from the earth. Then he sent forth a dove from him, to see if the waters had subsided from the face of the ground. But the dove found no place to set her foot, and she returned to him to the ark, for the waters were still on the face of the whole earth. So he put out his hand and took her and brought her into the ark with him. He waited another seven days, and again he sent forth the dove out of the ark. And the dove came back to him in the evening, and behold, in her mouth was a freshly plucked olive leaf. So Noah knew that the waters had subsided from the earth. Then he waited another seven days and sent forth the dove, and she did not return to him anymore" (Genesis 8:6-12).

With the waters subsiding, the raven, being unclean, may have discovered the corpses of men and animals and, finding nourishment there, did not return to the ark. The dove, being clean and with a more discriminating diet, found no acceptable nourishment among the death and rottenness left behind by the flood, and so returned to the ark. After seven days Noah sent the dove again, and this time the dove returned with evidence that the water had subsided and life had returned to an olive tree.

The Holy Spirit reveals truth about two kinds of disciples here. Both birds were saved from the flood by Noah's ark, but one, the raven, was so quickly and completely enticed away from the ark by the temptations of the old world of sin and death, that he was of no use to Noah. But the dove was not distracted by the same temptations and therefore was able to be focused on the task of finding and bringing evidence of fresh new life back to Noah. It's no wonder God chose the dove to identify His Son to John the Baptist and to the world... *"I saw the Spirit descend from heaven like a dove, and it remained on him"* (John 1:32).

Which bird reflects your availability to God? Are you so consumed by the world that you are unavailable to serve Him? How about the worldview of our children? Are they so filled with the foolishness of the world that they are unable to discern and follow the Holy Spirit's leading? As we *grow up into Christ* may we become more like the dove, set apart from the world, living above its temptation and decay, and available to serve The Lord. May we learn well this lesson from Noah about...

Ravens, Doves, and Serving God.

Go Out from the Ark

"In the six hundred and first year, in the first month, the first day of the month, the waters were dried from off the earth. And Noah removed the covering of the ark and looked, and behold, the face of the ground was dry. In the second month, on the twenty-seventh day of the month, the earth had dried out. Then God said to Noah, 'Go out from the ark, you and your wife, and your sons and your sons' wives with you. Bring out with you every living thing that is with you of all flesh—birds and animals and every creeping thing that creeps on the earth—that they may swarm on the earth, and be fruitful and multiply on the earth.' So Noah went out, and his sons and his wife and his sons' wives with him. Every beast, every creeping thing, and every bird, everything that moves on the earth, went out by families from the ark" (Genesis 8:13-19).

The Spirit reveals two important truths here. The first comes in God's command, *"Go out from the ark"* and the second in the manner in which the animals *"went out by families"*.

God used the ark to save Noah and his family from His judgment of the world's sin. He never intended for them to remain in the ark. They were to *"go out"* and change the world by repopulating it. The plan was for these righteous people to produce righteous children for generations to come. One day the Messiah who would be a blessing to the whole world would come through this line.

The animals that had entered the ark in *"pairs"* **(Genesis 7:2-3)** now went out *"by families"* from the ark. The ark had nurtured and produced life that would now go out into the world to repopulate it.

God's Word compels us here to go out into our world and make a difference for Christ. Like Noah, we have been saved from God's judgment of sin through Christ's blood and often the temptation is for us to remain inside the safe confines of the church, or to stay safe in the quiet intimacy of our walk with Jesus. But as we *grow up into Christ,* we remember that Jesus commanded us to *"Go into all the world and proclaim the gospel to the whole creation"* (Mark 16:15). Let's find a fresh way to share the good news somewhere in our world today as we...

Go Out from the Ark.

God Still Responds to Evil Hearts

"Then Noah built an altar to the Lord and took some of every clean animal and some of every clean bird and offered burnt offerings on the altar. And when the Lord smelled the pleasing aroma, the Lord said in his heart, 'I will never again curse the ground because of man, for the intention of man's heart is evil from his youth. Neither will I ever again strike down every living creature as I have done. While the earth remains, seedtime and harvest, cold and heat, summer and winter, day and night, shall not cease'" **(Genesis 8:20-22).**

The Spirit of Truth reveals the condition of human hearts here. The condition of Noah's heart and the condition of the hearts of men and women in general are exposed in Moses' record of the first moments on dry land after the great flood, and a critical truth about how God responds to our hearts is revealed.

Noah sacrificed some of the clean animals despite the natural fear that they should be used to repopulate the earth. If the plan was to fill the earth with life once again, wouldn't every possible animal saved on the ark be needed to accomplish the task? Noah's sacrifice revealed that he trusted the task of repopulating the earth to God. His heart was filled with and motivated by faith. His faithful action teaches us that we are to faithfully hear and obey God, trusting Him to lead and provide all we need to be a part of His perfect plan.

In today's text God openly declares truth about the condition of man's heart. He says the *intention* (Hebrew: yēṣer - *imagination, conception, frame of reference, worldview*) of our hearts is evil from our birth. Here is the evidence that we have inherited a sin nature from Adam. Here is evidence that while the world was changed by the flood, our hearts were not.

While the flood demonstrated God's judgment of sin, it was never meant to remove sin from the world because sin resides in the human heart. Therefore, God declares that He will not initiate a worldwide judgment of sin by the destruction of all life again. But, in accepting the sacrifice offered by a humble, faithful servant like Noah, God shows that He will respond with grace and forgiveness to all who approach Him in faith. The approach is still through a sacrifice provided by God Himself... *"Behold, the Lamb of God, who takes away the sin of the world!"* (John 1:29). As we *grow up into Christ* seeking and sharing His truth with others, we are ever more aware that...

God Still Responds to Evil Hearts.

God Values Life

"And God blessed Noah and his sons and said to them, 'Be fruitful and multiply and fill the earth. The fear of you and the dread of you shall be upon every beast of the earth and upon every bird of the heavens, upon everything that creeps on the ground and all the fish of the sea. Into your hand they are delivered. Every moving thing that lives shall be food for you. And as I gave you the green plants, I give you everything.

But you shall not eat flesh with its □life, that is, its blood. And for your lifeblood I will require a reckoning: from every beast I will require it and □from man. From his fellow man I will require a reckoning for the life of man. Whoever sheds the blood of man, by man shall his blood be shed, for God made man in his own image. And you, be fruitful and multiply, increase greatly on the earth and multiply in it'" (Genesis 9:1-7).

Today's scripture is full of truth about mankind because contained in a blessing upon Noah and his family is a declaration from God about the relationship between man and beast and the value of human life. And, the truth is revealed through a blessing from a Holy God to fallen man!

Sin had produced in man a diminished view of the value of life, of both animal and human life. God responded with a dramatic change after the flood that is revealed here. Man would still be God's steward and rule over the rest of the creatures, but because of sin and its consequences, God placed a fear of man in the animals. Creatures that once submitted to the loving care of Adam and Eve would now submit out of fear to mankind. And as a result of the fall, man would kill and eat the animals he was destined to care for. Perhaps God expected man, in his selfishness, to be more caring for animals that he now depended upon for food?

God's blessing went on to separate and elevate the value of human life above all other life. Human beings are different because *"God made man in His own image".* Therefore, when a human life was taken by man or beast there was a price that must be paid. The price was a life for a life, blood for blood.

God established an inescapable truth here. Sin causes death and death requires reckoning. Because we all have sinned (see Romans 3:23), we all deserve death (see Genesis 2:17). Our only hope to overcome death is in the reckoning death of the One God appointed to pay the price for our sin, Jesus Christ (see Romans 6:26). As we *grow up into Christ* may we be ever more thankful that Jesus valued our lives enough to die that we might live, and may we show the world that we understand how much...

God Values Life.

Children of the Covenant

"Then God said to Noah and to his sons with him, 'Behold, I establish my covenant with you and your offspring after you, and with every living creature that is with you, the birds, the livestock, and every beast of the earth with you, as many as came out of the ark; it is for every beast of the earth. I establish my covenant with you, that never again shall all flesh be cut off by the waters of the flood, and never again shall there be a flood to destroy the earth.' And God said, 'This is the sign of the covenant that I make between me and you and every living creature that is with you, for all future generations: I have set my bow in the cloud, and it shall be a sign of the covenant between me and the earth. When I bring clouds over the earth and the bow is seen in the clouds, I will remember my covenant that is between me and you and every living creature of all flesh. And the waters shall never again become a flood to destroy all flesh. When the bow is in the clouds, I will see it and remember the everlasting covenant between God and every living creature of all flesh that is on the earth.' God said to Noah, 'This is the sign of the covenant that I have established between me and all flesh that is on the earth'" (Genesis 9:8-17).

The Spirit of Truth teaches here that God's covenant with all living creatures was unconditional. Note that God's covenant was with *"every living creature".* Usually covenants are formed between two rational parties that are able to understand, agree to, and fulfill promises and conditions. The only living creature that could respond rationally was man. God was initiating a covenant where He made a unilateral promise that did not depend upon the understanding or acceptance of man or beast. This covenant prefigures the same unconditional love and grace of the new covenant that Jesus Christ initiated through His sacrifice on the cross... *"This cup that is poured out for you is the new covenant in my blood"* (Luke 22:20). The new covenant is unconditional in that believers do not have to meet any conditions or fulfill any promises beyond believing in Christ as Savior.

The rainbow God provided as a symbol of His promise teaches us the truth that God is sovereign over nature. The rainbow is caused by nature. In a rainbow, raindrops in the air act as tiny prisms. Light enters the raindrop, reflects off of the side of the drop and exits. In the process, it is broken into a spectrum just like it is in a triangular glass prism. God chose something that would occur often in the natural order he created to reinforce that although there will be storms on the earth, He will establish their boundaries and limit their destructive force. Truth seekers recognize the comforting truth of God's sovereignty over and protection through all the storms of life, whether they are physical, emotional, or spiritual.

Just as the covenant God made with Noah and his family was sealed with the natural symbol of the rainbow, the new covenant between Christ and believers is sealed with the natural symbols of Christ's body and blood, bread and wine. As we *grow up into Christ,* may the rainbow, bread, and wine remind us of God's unconditional love and protection toward us because we are...

Children of the Covenant.

The Pattern of Enslavement

"The sons of Noah who went forth from the ark were Shem, Ham, and Japheth. (Ham was the father of Canaan). These three were the sons of Noah, and from these the people of the whole earth were dispersed. Noah began to be a man of the soil, and he planted a vineyard. He drank of the wine and became drunk and lay uncovered in his tent. And Ham, the father of Canaan, saw the nakedness of his father and told his two brothers outside. Then Shem and Japheth took a garment, laid it on both their shoulders, and walked backward and covered the nakedness of their father. Their faces were turned backward, and they did not see their father's nakedness. When Noah awoke from his wine and knew what his youngest son had done to him, he said, 'Cursed be Canaan; a servant of servants shall he be to his brothers.' He also said, 'Blessed be the Lord, the God of Shem; and let Canaan be his servant. May God enlarge Japheth, and let him dwell in the tents of Shem, and let Canaan be his servant.' After the flood Noah lived 350 years. All the days of Noah were 950 years, and he died" **(Genesis 9:18-29).**

The Holy Spirit teaches important truth about wine, self-control, and respect here. Truth is revealed in the pattern of Noah's behavior and in his sons' reaction to his behavior. Note the pattern, *Noah drank wine, became drunk, and lay uncovered.*

The Bible, our ultimate authority, teaches much truth regarding the drinking of alcohol. God's Word does not forbid a Christian from drinking beer, wine, or any other drink containing alcohol. In fact, some Scriptures discuss alcohol in positive terms. Jesus changed water into wine **(John 2:1-11)**.It even seems that Jesus drank wine on occasion **(Matthew 26:29)**. Paul instructed Timothy to drink wine to help with a stomach ailment **(1 Timothy 5:23)**. At the same time, God's Word commands Christians to avoid drunkenness **(Ephesians 5:18).** The Bible condemns drunkenness and its effects **(Proverbs 23:29-35)**.Christians are also commanded to not allow their bodies to be "mastered" by anything **(1 Corinthians 6:12; 2 Peter 2:19)**. Drinking alcohol in excess or depending on alcohol to control emotional or mental health leads to addiction. God's Word also says Christians should not do anything that might offend other weaker Christians or cause them to sin against their own conscience **(1 Corinthians 8:9-13).**

Moses reports that God did not discipline Noah for *drinking wine*. However, Noah's *drunkenness* led to his complete loss of self-control and nakedness. God does not want His children to be enslaved to anything in this world... ***"For whatever overcomes a person, to that he is enslaved"*(2 Peter 2:19).** Noah's enslavement by alcohol led to the enslavement of Ham's descendants to the generation of his son Canaan and beyond.

The Holy Spirit teaches truth seekers here to be careful to not allow anything to master or enslave us. The same truth is echoed by the pen of the apostle Paul, ***"Do not get drunk with wine, for that is debauchery, but be filled with the Spirit"* (Ephesians 5:18).** As Christ followers we are to avoid anything that might prevent us from being filled with and led by the Holy Spirit. As we *grow up into Christ* may we be sensitive and resistant to people, philosophies, and things that might seek to enslave us and may we not be trapped by...

The Pattern of Enslavement.

The Only True King

"These are the generations of the sons of Noah, Shem, Ham, and Japheth. Sons were born to them after the flood. The sons of Japheth: Gomer, Magog, Madai, Javan, Tubal, Meshech, and Tiras. The sons of Gomer: Ashkenaz, Riphath, and Togarmah. The sons of Javan: Elishah, Tarshish, Kittim, and Dodanim. From these the coastland peoples spread in their lands, each with his own language, by their clans, in their nations.

The sons of Ham: Cush, Egypt, Put, and Canaan. The sons of Cush: Seba, Havilah, Sabtah, Raamah, and Sabteca. The sons of Raamah: Sheba and Dedan. Cush fathered Nimrod; he was the first on earth to be a mighty man. He was a mighty hunter before the LORD. Therefore it is said, "Like Nimrod a mighty hunter before the LORD." The beginning of his kingdom was Babel, Erech, Accad, and Calneh, in the land of Shinar. From that land he went into Assyria and built Nineveh, Rehoboth-Ir, Calah, and Resen between Nineveh and Calah; that is the great city. Egypt fathered Ludim, Anamim, Lehabim, Naphtuhim, Pathrusim, Casluhim (from whom the Philistines came), and Caphtorim. Canaan fathered Sidon his firstborn and Heth, and the Jebusites, the Amorites, the Girgashites, the Hivites, the Arkites, the Sinites, the Arvadites, the Zemarites, and the Hamathites. Afterward the clans of the Canaanites dispersed. And the territory of the Canaanites extended from Sidon in the direction of Gerar as far as Gaza, and in the direction of Sodom, Gomorrah, Admah, and Zeboiim, as far as Lasha. These are the sons of Ham, by their clans, their languages, their lands, and their nations. To Shem also, the father of all the children of Eber, the elder brother of Japheth, children were born.

The sons of Shem: Elam, Asshur, Arpachshad, Lud, and Aram. The sons of Aram: Uz, Hul, Gether, and Mash. Arpachshad fathered Shelah; and Shelah fathered Eber. To Eber were born two sons: the name of the one was Peleg, for in his days the earth was divided, and his brother's name was Joktan. Joktan fathered Almodad, Sheleph, Hazarmaveth, Jerah, Hadoram, Uzal, Diklah, Obal, Abimael, Sheba, Ophir, Havilah, and Jobab; all these were the sons of Joktan. The territory in which they lived extended from Mesha in the direction of Sephar to the hill country of the east. These are the sons of Shem, by their clans, their languages, their lands, and their nations. These are the clans of the sons of Noah, according to their genealogies, in their nations, and from these the nations spread abroad on the earth after the flood" (Genesis 10:1-32).

Such a long list of names! There are many geographical and historical facts revealed in the lists, like the origins of three branches of humanity and where they began to settle. But there is also important truth about the character of mankind to be mined here.

There is only one character with any biographical information included here. His name is Nimrod, and his name came to be associated with rebellion. Our text simply says that Nimrod *"was the first on earth to be a mighty man"* and he was *"He was a mighty hunter before the LORD".* On the surface, that sounds like a good report, but when we also consider that Nimrod's *kingdom* began in *Babel* we discover some not so positive truth about him.

Until Nimrod, there was no king beside God. People did not rule over one another. It appears God blessed Nimrod with great strength and excellent hunting skills, but instead of using them to serve others; he used them to exert power over others. The city he founded would soon be the birthplace of a large scale rebellion against God in the attempted construction of the Tower of Babel.

This brief description of Nimrod was included in God's Word by the Spirit of Truth to teach us that God has created and gifted each of us for His special purpose. This truth is echoed by the pen of the apostle Paul, *"We are his workmanship, created in Christ Jesus for good works, which God prepared beforehand, that we should walk in them"* (Ephesians **2:10).** We also learn here that we may use the special talent and gifts of God to build our own selfish little kingdom or to serve God and others in His kingdom. As we *grow up into Christ* may we earnestly serve...

The Only True King.

Nothing is Impossible!

"Now the whole earth had one language and the same words. And as people migrated from the east, they found a plain in the land of Shinar and settled there. And they said to one another, 'Come, let us make bricks, and burn them thoroughly.' And they had brick for stone, and bitumen for mortar. Then they said, 'Come, let us build ourselves a city and a tower with its top in the heavens, and let us make a name for ourselves, lest we be dispersed over the face of the whole earth.' And the Lord came down to see the city and the tower, which the children of man had built. And the Lord said, 'Behold, they are one people, and they have all one language, and this is only the beginning of what they will do. And nothing that they propose to do will now be impossible for them. Come, let us go down and there confuse their language, so that they may not understand one another's speech.' So the Lord dispersed them from there over the face of all the earth, and they left off building the city. Therefore its name was called Babel, because there the Lord confused the language of all the earth. And from there the Lord dispersed them over the face of all the earth" (Genesis 11:1-9).

What were they thinking? Let's outsmart God. We'll be ready for Him next time. Let's build a tower, a way of escape from any future flood. That's one sure way to keep people close by and together, under our rule. This thinking shows how quickly ambition clouded reason and erased the memory of God's promise, no more flood. But ambitious rulers manipulated and deceived unbelieving followers, and people used the gift of one language, given by God that they might communicate with and praise Him, for their own evil, ambitious purpose. They built a tower.

What was God to do? He expressed the truth that mankind, united and using the gifts He provided, is able to accomplish anything, be it good or evil. But He showed very clearly that He was in charge! He dispersed them and took away the gift of one language. God's Word reveals an important truth here. God will empower us to do great things only when our ambition is to please Him and we use His gifts for His purposes.

Of course this truth is not learned from the philosophy of the world, which teaches that we are ever evolving into higher life forms and still promotes the same Babylonian philosophy that man can do any selfish thing he sets his mind and talent to. Notice that building the Tower of Babel began with the rejection of God's spoken truth, a promise that He will never again destroy the world with a flood.

The Biblical truth is that truth followers can do great things because, *"with God all things are possible"* **(Matthew 19:26).** The Biblical truth that we and our children, (God's kids) will learn only from truth seeking and believing teachers is, *"I can do all things through Christ who strengthens me"* **(Philippians 4:13, NKJV).** As we *grow up into Christ* may we be encouraged by the truth that in Him...

Nothing is Impossible!

Our Sure Hope

"These are the generations of Shem. When Shem was 100 years old, he fathered Arpachshad two years after the flood. And Shem lived after he fathered Arpachshad 500 years and had other sons and daughters. When Arpachshad had lived 35 years, he fathered Shelah. And Arpachshad lived after he fathered Shelah 403 years and had other sons and daughters. When Shelah had lived 30 years, he fathered Eber. And Shelah lived after he fathered Eber 403 years and had other sons and daughters. When Eber had lived 34 years, he fathered Peleg. And Eber lived after he fathered Peleg 430 years and had other sons and daughters. When Peleg had lived 30 years, he fathered Reu. And Peleg lived after he fathered Reu 209 years and had other sons and daughters. When Reu had lived 32 years, he fathered Serug. And Reu lived after he fathered Serug 207 years and had other sons and daughters. When Serug had lived 30 years, he fathered Nahor. And Serug lived after he fathered Nahor 200 years and had other sons and daughters. When Nahor had lived 29 years, he fathered Terah. And Nahor lived after he fathered Terah 119 years and had other sons and daughters. When Terah had lived 70 years, he fathered Abram, Nahor, and Haran. Now these are the generations of Terah. Terah fathered Abram, Nahor, and Haran; and Haran fathered Lot. Haran died in the presence of his father Terah in the land of his kindred, in Ur of the Chaldeans" (Genesis 11:10-28).

Today's text reveals the truth that God fulfills His promises. This truth offers us a sure hope, no matter what's going on around us. In the midst of the dismal events of Genesis 3-11, the Spirit of truth moved Moses to record the line of descendants from Shem to Abram. Here, hope emerges from the darkness and judgments of the fall, the flood, and the tower. Just after the record of confusion and rebellion surrounding the Tower of Babel, constructed by the descendants of Ham, God's Word redirects our focus to Abram, a descendant of Shem and *"The father of all who believe"* (Romans 4:11). It was through Abram (later Abraham) that God would bless all nations and the promised Messiah would come. The line of

106

Shem would produce the children of Israel and those who by faith look to Jesus Christ, the citizens of Augustine's "city of God".

Today's text encourages us to put our hope in the Lord, no matter how hopeless the world around us appears. The blessings for those who hope in the Lord are many. Among them are the promise that *"the eye of the Lord is on those who fear Him, on those who hope in His steadfast love"* **(Psalm 33:18)**, *and "the Lord takes pleasure in those who fear Him, in those who hope in His steadfast love"* **(Psalm 147:11).** Finally, as we *grow up into Christ,* we are to *"renounce ungodliness and worldly passions, and to live self-controlled, upright, and godly lives in the present age, waiting for our blessed hope, the appearing of the glory of our great God and Savior Jesus Christ"* **(Titus 2:12-13).** We can fix our hope on Christ because God's Word proves over and over again that Jesus Christ is indeed...

Our Sure Hope.

Prepared for Greatness

"And Abram and Nahor took wives. The name of Abram's wife was Sarai, and the name of Nahor's wife, Milcah, the daughter of Haran the father of Milcah and Iscah. Now Sarai was barren; she had no child. Terah took Abram his son and Lot the son of Haran, his grandson, and Sarai his daughter-in-law, his son Abram's wife, and they went forth together from Ur of the Chaldeans to go into the land of Canaan, but when they came to Haran, they settled there. The days of Terah were 205 years, and Terah died in Haran" (Genesis 11:29-32).

These first eleven chapters of the Bible come to a close with a focus on a tough time in the life of a young man named Abram. The genealogies all stream to Abram. The action is all about Abram's small family and migration to Haran. The story ends with the death of Abram's father, the bareness of Abram's wife, and the failure of Abram's mission to reach Canaan. It was a humbling moment for Abram, but the truth is God was preparing him for a very great part in His big plan!

Upon the death of his father, Abram assumed the role of patriarch in this young family. The death of his brother Haran in Ur and the decision of his brother Nahor to remain in Ur left no competition for leadership of the clan. Though Abram did not seek it, God had established him now as the authority over his family, and he was in position to follow God's lead and bring his family along with him.

Terah died while the family delayed and set up housekeeping in the land of Haran, short of the goal of the land of Canaan. This was a clear warning to Abram to get the family back on track with the Lord's plan to move on to Canaan. Abram was learning that rejecting the will of God leads to death, while there is life in pursuing *"the will of God, what is good and acceptable and perfect"* (Romans 12:2).

Finally, the Spirit of Truth records the barrenness of Sarai, Abram's wife here. Remember, God's ultimate purpose here is to preserve the line of the Messiah, the One who will crush the head of the serpent. All of

Satan's energies and schemes have been to destroy this line in a fruitless effort to prevent the fulfillment of God's plan. Abram would have to trust in God's supernatural providence if he hoped to have any children at all.

While on the surface, Abram appears to be in a very bleak place, he is in truth, in the perfect place. He is in the center of the will of God, and God is preparing him for greatness by humbling him and making him sensitive and responsive to God's providence and grace. As we *grow up into Christ,* may we be thankful for those humbling moments when the truth is, in God's perfect way, we are being...

Prepared for Greatness!

Made in the USA
Charleston, SC
04 May 2013